The
Second
Scar

A Journey
of
Survival

ISBN: 978-1-7343827-7-8

Library of Congress Control Number: 2023900562

Drawings for this book: Nikki Basch Davis
Website: nikkibaschdavis.com

Book design: Jan Malin

Cover image: Lena and Ama Goldberg,
mother and daughter

Published by CANYON ROSE PRESS
Benicia, California
email: info@canyonrosepress.com

The
Second
Scar

*A Journey
of
Survival*

Nechama Goldberg

Dedication

To my mother, Lena Goldberg, who through the first five years of my life, by personal example, taught me how to be brave, adventurous, committed and loyal.

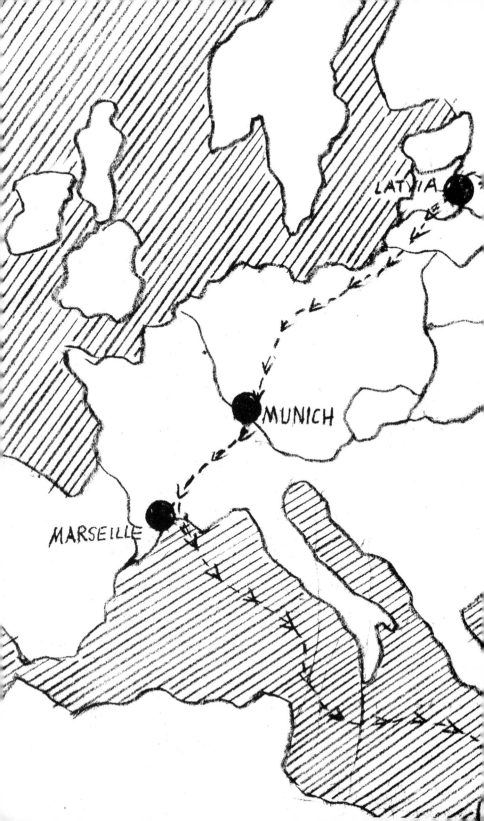

The Journey

Foreword

Nechama Goldberg's powerful memoir, *The Second Scar*, begins in the years before World War II disrupts her family's peaceful Latvian home-town. Caught between the Soviet occupiers and the Nazi invaders, millions of Jews across the Baltic States, Goldbergs' family among them, have no choice but to flee for their lives.

Because she was an infant when her family initially fled, Goldberg chooses to tell her story in the third person, weaving together her mother's recollections with bits of her own memories, as the child gradually becomes conscious of her surroundings.

When we first meet Nechama, known as "Ama," in the book's Prologue, she is barely more than a toddler, but already she knows to fear abandonment.

Cheated out of a childhood that should have been rooted and peaceful, little Ama comes to a consciousness of herself—of her identity and where she belongs as a displaced person.

Ama leaves her hometown as a babe in arms, losing her father before she could even begin to know him. Her mother, Lena, is the only constant in her life.

By the time Ama can begin to think and form memories for herself, she understands that anyone she loves can disappear in the blink of an eye. She learns not only that the world is not rational, but that it is full of arbitrary tragedy and determined evil.

Lena, who has already experienced too much traumatic loss in her young life, wanted to emigrate to the Jewish homeland with her elder brothers well before the Nazis arrived, but, as a daughter, she was expected to stay and care for her parents and younger brother.

As Lena pursues her dangerous travels with her child, Israel is always in her thoughts as a perfect refuge, a utopia that seems out of reach but even this ideal does not live up to her or Ama's needs and hopes for a new home.

Lena, irreparably damaged by her ordeal, is unable to bond with the daughter she loves so intensely. After so much sacrifice, Lena cannot let go of the unyielding control that allowed her to save both their lives. Joy and affection have become difficult for her. Even when a person survives it, such deep suffering leaves it's scar.

This story of courage, of harrowing loss, and of a mother's fierce determination to keep her child safe, is told with a clear-eyed recognition of human strength and weakness, cruelty and kindness, at times with humor, but also with the lasting bitterness of refugees who arrive at what they think is a safe haven, only to discover that, as refugees, they are not welcome.

As we watch people displaced by war and poverty seek refuge in our present day, *The Second Scar* serves as a timely call to compassion and a reminder that those who do not learn from history are doomed to repeat it.

Mary Eichbauer

Mary Eichbauer, Ph.D., has taught Humanities, English, and Women's Studies. Publications include a book of literary criticism, scholarly articles, book reviews and a book of poetry, *After the Opera*.

Contents

Preface

I chose to write this book under a pen name out of respect for the memory of two amazing women, my mother Lena Goldberg and my grandmother Nechama Goldberg, after whom I was named and who I only knew through my mother's stories.

A second reason was that during the period this book describes the girl in the story was called Nechama Goldberg. I wanted to write it in her voice.

Most of these stories were told to me as I sat at the table in my mother's kitchen. She talked, and I filed her words away in my memory. Some of these stories are also based on my own childhood recollections. Later I told these stories to my own children.

For many years I thought these memories illustrated how my mother saved my life. Later I understood that we saved each other's lives— my mother by being the fearless lioness and me by giving her the primal reason for survival, to save her child's life.

Now that I have transferred these memories into a book, I hope that these stories will be shared around other kitchen tables.

In writing *The Second Scar* I was telling a story that was hidden and untold for decades, mostly because I felt that, maybe, not speaking of those experiences would diminish them. I still tend not to share, not talk about hurtful or worrisome experiences until the gravity dissipates, feeling that sharing might make it more real.

That's what happened with Ama's first five years. She never talked about those years, as if the silence will erase the experience. Her aim was not to stand out as different. She wanted to blend, to become one of them, one of the cool Sabras (Sabra is the Hebrew name for the cactus plant. The native born were given the nickname to describe their nature, sweet on the inside, thorny on the outside). Her foreign Russian accent soon disappeared. She learned the good phrases and the local swear words. Her desire was to blend, and so she did.

The surviving Jews immigrating to Israel were often made to feel shame. It was subtle but embedded in the culture of the young vibrant society determined to fight for its existence and never again be displaced, humiliated, and slaughtered. The new generation in Israel, learning of the atrocities that their fellow men and women suffered, displayed either disbelief or judgment. Their understanding of the circumstances was limited. The query was: "why didn't you fight? Why were you led to slaughter like mindless sheep?" Ama wanted no part of that image, and she turned her back on her early years.

Nikki Basch Davis

Prologue

She slept with her mother, her sleep deep and peaceful, her legs draped over her mother's body, making sure she would not wake up alone to find herself left behind.

The barn, their refuge for the night, was cozy. Being warm was a luxury. Three-year-old Ama was traveling with her mother, riding in drafty train cars or trekking by foot along windy roads, searching for a place to rest for the night. It was early spring. The temperature, in the low 40s, was showing no mercy to the homeless.

There was an earthy smell of hay and animals in the barn. No sounds came from the main house. No one was in a hurry to do their daily chores. The elderly couple occupying the farmhouse were still recovering from long hours of work they endured the day before.

When Ama woke up her mother was gone. It was barely morning. A faint light signaling dawn was gaining over the night. A soft sound of bleating came from the sheep stall. They were ready to be milked.

Ama, discovering her mother's absence, leaped off the pile of hay that was their bed for the night. Whimpering, she inched towards the barn door. She swept the field with her eyes, frantically looking for her mother. Cold fear gripped her heart. The tattered nightdress she wore stuck to her little body. The air was cool, but she was perspiring. She took quick shallow breaths. Her mother was nowhere to be seen.

She froze with fear and took a hesitant step, venturing outside the barn. She was barefoot. The rough dirt hurt the soles of her little feet, but she felt nothing, only a sinking feeling of dread in the pit of her stomach. Lena walked among the orchard trees. She was wrapped in a woolen shawl. The air was crisp and cool. The scent of blossoms from the trees was strong. She heard soft whimpering and saw her daughter wandering through the trees, clutching a tattered old blanket to her body. There was fear on her little face. Lena ran towards her, bent down, and whispered "Amichka, did I frighten you? I am sorry, my love. I will never leave you behind, I promise."

Lena scooped up her daughter in her arms and kept wandering through the orchard. The fruit on the trees had not yet ripened. Hunger had no preference. Lena inched quietly towards the apple trees. She picked as much of the unripe fruit as her pockets could carry, not considering that later, eating the green fruit could make her ill. She was careful to be silent and not get caught by the owners. They were kind people. They had opened their home to her and her daughter and let them spend the night in their barn. Stealing their fruit was not a thing she ordinarily would do, but these were different times. This was war. The rules had changed. Only survival mattered.

1

Words are not birds; they don't fly away

Moshe Goldberg was a cloth merchant in a small town in Latvia named Rēzekne. The town had a large thriving Jewish population. Moshe owned a fabric store that supplied the Jews and Gentiles with fabric goods for their homes and farms. He was an industrious man and worked hard to provide for his large family.

Moshe and his wife, Nechama, lived in a modest home he had built with the helping hands of people from the community. It was small but adequate for his family.

Life at the Goldbergs' home was generally calm and congenial. Nechama handled a large household: her husband, Moshe; her three sons, Eli, Ari, and Ilka; her daughter, Lena; and her elderly mother, Rachel, who lived in an adjacent cottage Moshe had built specially for her.

They relied on a well for their water supply. It was Lena's duty to bring a fresh bucket of water into the house every morning for their cooking needs. Once a week, her brothers brought in large amounts of water from the well for their weekly baths. The small outhouse in the corner of their property was often in great demand, being shared by six family members.

Moshe and Nechama were distinguished members of the Jewish community. She was known for her wit and kind heart. There were many impoverished families in town, and she did her share to ensure they had food and shelter. On Fridays,

Nechama would visit Jewish homes of the less fortunate families and deliver food items for the traditional Shabbat dinner, items she collected from homes of wealthier families. When she was asked "Who is this food going to?" she would answer with a smile, "Your duty is just to give," ensuring that no one was shamed by gossip.

Nechama's good nature balanced Moshe's bad moods, which were fueled by his frequent bouts with migraines. He could become short and angry at the drop of a hat. The children learned to stay out of his way. When he turned on his wife with abusive words she would answer, "Moishe, words are not birds, they don't fly away." Her innate wisdom would eventually calm him down.

2

A harrowing experience,
but not entirely wasted

A grand river ran near their home, the Rēzekne river. It was a favorite place for youth to gather. Latvia was blessed with temperate weather. On warm days they would swim and linger on its sunny shores. Eli, at 16, and Ari, at 14, were among those youths. The river was wide and deep and known for its strong currents. Lena, at 12, was always eager to join them, but they were not so eager to have her tag along and kept trying to sneak out without her knowledge

One crisp June day she decided to go and look for them. She put on her bathing suit under her dress and headed for the river. Approaching, she heard sounds of laughter in the distance. The youngsters were obviously having fun. Looking through the limbs of a tree, she saw her brothers and their friends. They had swum across the river and gathered on its opposite shore. If she was to join them, she had to swim across.

"I can do it," she murmured to herself. "I'll show those two losers that I can be just as much fun," she thought. "Their friends are really cute, especially the one with the beautiful gray eyes."

The water was cold, and it took a few tries to immerse her whole body. She knew how to float, but she was not a strong swimmer.

Paddling with her arms and frog kicking her legs, she tried to look as elegant as possible, in case the boys glanced in her direction. Reaching the middle of the river, she felt the current veering her away from where she was headed. It was strong, and soon she was losing ground and beginning to drift. She couldn't stay afloat. In the grip of fear, she panicked. Her legs froze, and soon she began to sink, while yelling for help, as the water engulfed her. It took a few moments for the boys on the opposite bank to notice her flailing figure in the water and hear her screams.

She felt strong arms grip her as she was dragged to the riverbank. When she opened her eyes, she saw the worried face of a boy with beautiful gray eyes gazing down at her with great concern. It was the boy she secretly admired. She was still holding on to his neck and in no hurry to let go.

"Are you all right?" he asked, "It scared me when I saw you sink under."

"Thank you for saving me," she murmured, fluttering her eyelashes, hoping that her hair was not plastered to her head. "It was a harrowing experience, but not entirely wasted," she thought.

3

They were free to practice their religion

Rēzekne is a small town in eastern Latvia situated in the Rēzekne River Valley. Known as the city of seven hills, Rēzekne is nearly 150 miles east of Latvia's capital, Riga, 39 miles east of the Russian border, and 240 miles north of the Lithuanian border. As a result of these proximities, throughout history, the town was invaded and occupied multiple times by Lithuanian and Russian forces. The extensive railroad system crossing through town allowed easy access to other parts of the state and made it a desirable stronghold.

Before World War II, Rēzekne had become a cultural and economic center of the region. It attracted vacationers, drawn to its beauty. The city was surrounded by gardens, with the Rēzekne River meandering through town. Nearby lakes and forests added to its charm.

At least 60 percent of the town's population were Jews. It was one of the most important Jewish communities in Latvia. The community flourished. Children attended schools and were allowed to be taught the Hebrew language, free to practice their religion and teach it to their children. That freedom was taken away by the Soviet occupation in 1940. The Russian educational system was based on strict political and ideological principles. Its main goal was to instill in the population a total obedience towards their occupiers.

4

Nechama did command respect

Riga, Latvia's capital, was a fascinating city. Its rich architecture clearly showed that several cultures converged in this town. An abundance of merchandise from major European cities drew crowds of shoppers from neighboring towns.

It was early fall. Lena and her mother were on a train heading 148 miles west to Riga. It was their custom to take seasonal excursions to the capitol, purchasing clothes and household items for the family. The trips were also fruitful when Nechama needed fashionable attire.

From an early age, Lena accompanied her mother on her shopping trips to Riga. She loved these trips and watched with fascination the passing views through the train's window.

Latvia was blessed with picturesque sights. Flatlands alternated with hills. Lakes and rivers crisscrossed the countryside. Stately forests and expansive, lush meadows were all part of the Latvian landscape's unique mosaic.

Lena adored her mother and treasured the times she got to spend alone with her. They would dress in their finest clothes; Nechama's mood, once she was away from her daily chores, was light and gay. They had stayed overnight at a guest house. When morning came, they ventured into town to embark on their shopping spree.

Mother and daughter entered a millinery shop situated in Riga's fashionable district. The shop served women of high social standing who could afford its exorbitant prices.

The shopkeeper was a diminutive woman. She eyed the new patrons with an inquisitive eye and discerned immediately their social status and financial abilities. She hurried to their side. "How can I be of help my lady?" asked the small woman, bowing.

Nechama did command respect. She was a handsome woman. In her thirties, she carried her tall, ample figure with grace; her broad, Slavic face did not resemble the customary features of her tribe. Her deep brown eyes, when not weighed down by the burden of her life's responsibilities, seemed whimsical and inquisitive. She liked people, and they, in turn, were drawn to her.

Lena, standing by her mother's side, was struck by the beauty around her. Hats of all sizes, colors, and designs were perched on stands. They were adorned with feathers, ribbons, and fine gauzy material. She looked up and was met by her mother's smile.

"We are looking for a beautiful, elegant hat for a twelve-year-old girl," answered Nechama. "She is going to have a celebration of her Bat Mitzva in a month and she needs a hat to go with the blue silk dress she is going to wear." Lena's breath caught in her throat. The celebration for her Bat Mitzva was around the corner. Blue silk, from her father's shop, was selected for her dress, to be designed and tailored by a local seamstress. The purchase of a hat was a surprise.

Lena and her mother walked out of the shop hand in hand. Lena's face was beaming. On her head perched an exquisite white felt hat adorned with blue silk ribbons.

5

Go out there with your head held high

Rachel, Nechama's mother, suffered from an advanced case of arthritis. She was confined to her bed and had difficulties using her hands. Her condition didn't rob her of her wit and humor, which she had bequeathed to her daughter.

Rachel and her granddaughter, Lena, loved each other and found a common language despite the age difference. Lena visited her grandmother each day, bringing her the daily newspaper and keeping her company. They would catch up on the latest events around town, laugh, and exchange gossip.

One Friday morning, Lena entered her grandmother's bedroom carrying branches of fragrant blossoms that filled the room with scent. "Hello, my sweet girl," the old woman said in greeting. "What great news did you bring me today?"

"Mama is getting ready for the holidays, Eli is being his usual pesky self, and our trees are blossoming beautifully. I brought you some of the branches so you can enjoy their fragrance. I'll put them in water," answered Lena.

"And what's new with you, my sweet?" inquired the old lady.

Life is good," answered Lena. "I was promoted to group leader in my troop. I hope I can do the job. I am afraid I won't be able to do what's required of me. I can be quite an airhead at times."

"Listen to me," said Rachel in a stern voice. "Don't you put yourself down, you hear? There is a whole world out there that will be happy to do it for you. Don't you diminish your value. Walk out there with your head held high. Remember that you are a member of a special tribe. If you believe it, the rest of the world will follow."

Lena lowered her gaze. Her grandmother was wise and had a strong belief in her granddaughter's abilities, which Lena wasn't sure she shared.

"I see a new sparkle in your eyes," continued Rachel. "Was it placed there by a new boy in your life?" she asked with a wink.

Lena smiled. Grandma Rachel was blessed with a keen ability to observe and discern human behavior. Her love for her granddaughter and concern for her wellbeing were apparent to Lena. She trusted her grandmother with her secrets and liked to listen to her advice. "Too soon to tell, *Bube*, (Grandma)but you will be the first to know, I promise," she answered with a smile.

They settled companionably, sipped their morning tea, and discussed the latest happenings in their community. "So, how is your Tate (Father)?" Grandma Rachel inquired. "Is he suffering from headaches often? Is he hard on your Mama?"

"Mom knows how to handle him," answered Lena with a smile. "She gets him out of his moods quickly."

"*Bubale* (Sweetie)," said Rachel. "Can you bring me something from the bottom drawer of my bureau? There is a small black lacquered box. Bring it to me, please."

Lena placed the small, worn box next to her grandmother's shaky hand. Rachel opened the box and took out an exquisite gold ring with olive-green stones ornately set in an intricate design. "Here, my love, try this on," she said to Lena. "Your *zeyde* (Grandfather), Nathan, gave it to me when we got engaged." The ring was made for a small hand and fit Lena's finger perfectly.

"It looks so much better on your lovely hand than lying useless in a box. Take it and wear it in good health."

Lena bent down to hug her grandmother and kissed her softly on the cheek. "This is the most beautiful thing anyone has ever given me," she whispered. "I will treasure it forever and make sure that my daughters and granddaughters will know whose ring this was."

Rachel wrapped herself with her woolen shawl. It was a crisp, cool morning. She looked at her beautiful granddaughter with loving eyes. "Go, live your life, my child. I need to rest," she said and reclined back on her soft pillows.

6

They sang nostalgic, longing songs of hope for a glorious future

Lena's two older brothers, Eli and Ari, were active in the Zionist youth movement that prepared them for life in a new country, a country they believed was a homeland for the Jewish people. They were planning to go with the fifth wave of Jews heading for Palestine in the late 1930s. Their intention was to join in the efforts to revive a barren land and build a future homeland for unwanted, expelled, and displaced Jews.

Zionism was founded in the late 1800s by an Austrian Jew named Theodor Herzl. The movement's aim was to reestablish a Jewish national state, a home for the Jewish people.

Lena's circle of friends chose to follow a different faction of Zionism. "Beitar" originated in Riga, Latvia, established by Zeev Zabotinsky. Founding the revisionist movement was Zabotinsky's response to the persecution of Jews in Europe. He was responsible for spreading Hebrew language and culture throughout Europe. The followers of his movement were instructed on how to organize self-defense units to fight for Jewish rights. Zabotinsky's teachings aimed at infusing his followers with a militant and nationalistic spirit, which appealed to Lena, who was the fiery, feisty member of the Goldberg family.

One day Lena walked into the outhouse that was nestled on the edge of their property and found, to her disgust, a portrait of her revered leader hanging on its wall. Eli's smirk at the breakfast table revealed who was behind the prank.

Despite the differences in their political pursuits, the young members of the Goldberg family were dreaming of the same future, a future that had them settling into a life of freedom and pride in a new state, a Jewish state.

Ilia was a close friend of Lena's brothers. He was the boy that had jumped into the river to save Lena from the sweeping current when they were much younger. He was a quiet gentle soul. His love of music made him popular among the young people. They would gather outdoors on warm nights, sit around a fire, and dream of a sweet future when they'd be taking part in the creation of a proud existence, not as a despised minority, but as people free of fear of persecution. They sang nostalgic, longing songs of hope for a glorious future, accompanied by Ilia playing his accordion.

Lena, now in her early twenties, would join her brothers on those nights. She was drawn to the handsome young man whose grey eyes followed her movements, and his sweet voice raised in song seemed to be addressed mainly to her. He was her first love, and it was powerful. Ilia was a shy, reserved young man. The beautiful fair-haired young woman captured his heart. He fell in love with Lena.

The youth movements prepared the young men and women for their future. They were taught carpentry, welding, and electricity. They were also trained in building an agricultural farm in a small field near Riga. These skills were not taught to boys growing up in small, sheltered towns.

The time for Eli, Ari, and Ilia to embark on their journey arrived. The parting was heavy and sorrowful. No one knew when they would see each other again.

Lena desperately wanted to join them, but their parents could not be left alone to handle two households and a thriving store. She, the daughter, was the obvious choice to stay and carry the burden of their care. She understood her traditional role but was left with some measure of resentment.

Lena and Ilia were in love. They dreamed of a future together and planned to start a new life in an exciting new country. They met the night before Ilia's departure and spent it in each other's arms, whispering encouraging promises to wait faithfully until they reunited. Ilia pulled a small box out of his pocket and placed a simple silver ring on Lena's finger. "With this ring I promise to wait until we can start a life as a husband and wife," he whispered. They got engaged before his departure and planned to meet soon in the promised land. Lena's plan was to join the young men as soon as possible. She yearned to become part of this new historical adventure.

The next morning Lena and her mother accompanied the lads to the train station. They waited for a train that would take them to Riga. Nechama held on to her two older sons in a tight embrace. She was proud of the future they chose but heartbroken to see them go. Lena carried a bag of food she had prepared for each of them. She placed the bags in their hands, embraced each of them in turn and quickly departed.

7

The bird was perched on the kitchen windowsill

Life at the Goldberg's home was never the same. The sounds of banter and laughter among the siblings were gone. Lena continued, dutifully helping her father in his fabric store and her mother with the care of the home and her frail grandmother.

It was a fall day. Lena's feelings of gloom were intensified by the weather. She looked out the window of their kitchen as if expecting someone's arrival. She sighed and turned towards the door. "I will go down to the root cellar to fetch some fresh vegetables," she said to her mother. They were preparing the meals for the day.

"No, darling, you take Grandma Rachel her breakfast. You know how much she looks forward to spending this time with you. I will fetch the food."

Peering through the kitchen window, waiting for the breakfast porridge for her grandmother to be cooked, Lena noticed a white dove. The bird was perched on the kitchen windowsill. It trained its beady eyes insistently on Lena. "What?" asked Lena quietly. "Are you bringing me a message? I will get you some breadcrumbs as soon as I am done cooking."

Nechama proceeded towards their underground root cellar where they stored fruits and vegetables. She pulled the heavy cellar door, propped it open, and carefully started descending the ladder.

She heard a creak and looked up. The cellar door, old and in need of repair, pulled off its hinges, collapsed on her head, and knocked her to the ground.

She never recovered from her injuries. Five days later she passed away. Moshe lost his wife and Lena lost her mother. Nechama was 43 years old. The whole community mourned her untimely death.

Rachel, Lena's grandmother, never recovered from the loss of her daughter. "Children are not supposed to die before their parents," she muttered. She became withdrawn and sad. Lena couldn't revive her playful spirit. A couple of months after Nechama's death, Grandma Rachel died peacefully in her sleep.

With the loss of her mother and grandmother and her brothers gone to Palestine, Lena was left to care for her grieving father and her younger brother, Ilka. Her plans to follow Ilia and her brothers to Palestine were placed on an indefinite hold. Her father, Moshe, was not keen on the idea of uprooting and starting a new life in a faraway land. He was attached to his store, his home, and the familiar way of life. He felt tired and lonely after the death of his wife. He retreated to a life of work and frequent visits to the town's synagogue. The atmosphere of reverence and contemplation made him feel closer to his departed wife while he grieved.

Lena felt trapped. She yearned to grab a backpack and embark on a journey to join Ilia and her brothers, but she couldn't desert her father in his time of grief.

Months passed. Receiving mail from far away continents took as long as twelve weeks. News from Ilia and her brothers was sporadic.

The winter was cold that year. The rain seemed relentless. Lena's somber mood matched the weather. She was attending to her morning chores. The lilac trees had shed their bright red leaves. She was sweeping the front steps when she heard a dove's coo and raised her eyes to a tall branch. The white bird looked familiar. A feeling of dread filled Lena's heart. "Don't be silly," she reproached herself. "Don't go there. It's just a bird. I'll go get some stale breadcrumbs from the kitchen," she thought.

"Lena!" She heard her name called. Through the kitchen window she saw their mailman, Yoske, approaching the house. She hoped for a letter from Palestine, maybe from her brothers and, hopefully, from Ilia. The news they shared with her about their lives was a ray of sunshine in her gloomy existence. Her brothers lived in two newly established settlements. Eli was in charge of raising chickens and Ari was developing fishponds for raising carp. Ilia was employed in a school near Jerusalem, teaching young children how to plow and seed the land. The pictures they attached to their letters showed suntanned young men in work clothes with broad smiles on their faces.

Yoske smiled at the young woman and waved a letter. The blue envelope with the foreign-looking stamp was indeed from Palestine. It was from her older brother, Eli. He was the one who most diligently kept in touch with the family they had left behind. "Lenushka," Eli's letter began. "I am so sorry to write you this very grave news. It is about Ilia."

Britain was granted a mandate to rule over the countries of Palestine and Transjordan, "until such time as they are able to stand alone," the document declared. This decision was approved by the League of Nations. It was meant to be a transitional trusteeship to prepare Palestine to be a national home for the Jews without impairing the civil and religious rights of the indigenous Arab people who had also found a home in this land.

In the late 1930s, an Arab uprising began against the British administration, demanding an end to the policy of open-ended Jewish immigration and land purchases with the stated goal of establishing a Jewish national homeland.

The young and able men, arriving in Palestine with plans to revive the land, were met with fierce opposition. They found themselves in a struggle to reclaim their historic birthplace. Jews and Arabs entered a cycle of attacks and counterattacks. The young Jewish settlers resorted to learning how to fight back for their own protection. The training had to be done in hiding. Possession of arms and training in their use were against the law established by the ruling British authorities. Ilia's group was captured. They were discovered in possession of arms in the basement of a deserted building on the outskirts of Jerusalem.

Ilia's group was tried and sentenced to execution by hanging. The news hit Lena hard. A joyous adventure of three young men had turned into a tragic, dangerous reality. She mourned the death of the man she loved and became fearful for the lives of her brothers, Eli and Ari. She yearned to join them. She wanted to go and see the place that took the life of the man she loved; however, as the daughter, tradition dictated that she stay home and take care of her widowed parent. Lena had no means of escape.

Ilia's death left Lena depressed and mournful. The home she loved so much became a prison. Her young spirit ached for a life that had meaning and purpose, but none of that seemed to be part of her existence now. Most of the young men she knew had left for Palestine. She was taking care of her father's needs at home and in the family's fabric shop. One day chased another, and she couldn't see any exciting possibilities in her future.

8

My name is Micha Cherfas

One Friday morning, Lena stood behind her father's shop counter, folding large bolts of fabric left undone from the day before. It was winter. Christmas was around the corner. The town was decorated with lights. Storefronts showcased winter attire, and traditional Christmas music enticed shoppers to go inside. Families were strolling the avenues carrying large, colorful packages, and couples strolled hand in hand.

Lena's mood was somber. She was lonely, wondering if this was all she could look forward to in her life. The joyous, fun-loving girl had vanished. After the loss of her beloved mother, the departure of her brothers, and the death of the man she loved, life didn't have much to offer. Ilka, the youngest brother, was still at home. Due to the six-year difference in their ages—Ilka was only seventeen—they didn't share much more than meals and the care of their father and their home. Moshe, still grief stricken from the accident that took his wife's life, needed Lena's help in the shop. His zest and energy were waning.

She was alone, standing behind the counter, when the door to the shop opened and a tall young man walked in. It was unusual for men to frequent her father's shop. Women were mostly his patrons, purchasing cloth to make clothes for the family and decorate their homes. The man looked familiar. Rēzekne was a small town. She recognized many people by sight. They saw each other at high holidays, or when celebrating and praying at the local synagogue.

"My name is Micha Cherfas," he said while extending his hand to her in greeting.

Puzzled, she shook his hand and asked: "How can I help you? Would you like a lovely, printed fabric for a summer dress?" There was mischief in her smile. A sense of humor was an inherent quality in the women of the Goldberg family. The ice was broken. His stiff formal manner softened and was replaced by a warm, charming smile.

"Actually," he said, "I didn't come here for the merchandise. I came for the salesperson."

"Oh!" exclaimed Lena. "That would be me. What can I offer you?"

"Maybe a stroll in our city's park?" answered Micha. He didn't possess a classical beauty, but he had an open, kind face with a disarming smile. He knew her history and the fact that she had become reclusive since the death of her fiancé. He realized that he wasn't quite as dashing or young as the men whose passionate nature had driven them to leave their birth land and seek a new life. He was aware that he might not be quite as exciting to this beautiful young woman.

Lena considered Micha's words. She stared at him for a long while, not knowing what to make of his proposal. He was at least ten years her senior and seemed to exist in such a different reality than hers. She couldn't think of anything that they might have in common.

Micha could see the hesitation in her blue eyes. His heart was set on winning her trust. He cocked his head to one side and extended his hand to her. Lena responded and placed her hand lightly in his and was led by him from behind the counter.

They stood close, facing each other. Lena raised her face and met his eyes.

"All I am hoping for is a stroll in our city's park with a lovely young lady," he said softly. "I will bring you back safe and sound, I promise."

Lena responded with a smile. A first one in many days. "I guess that is innocent enough," she replied. "Although, in our little town, gossip spreads like fire. They'll see us walking side by side and they'll start naming our babies."

Micha chuckled heartily. She liked the way his face lit up when he smiled. "We'll keep a safe distance from each other," he said. "They are good people with too much idle time on their hands. They mean well."

"Most of the time," mused Lena, thinking of her two spinster aunts, her father's sisters. "Well," she said slowly, "I do feel stifled with only the store and the care of our father and our home as my daily chores. Going for walks with you might brighten my days, but," she continued, "I am not a good candidate for a romantic relationship right now, so if that's your intention, I will disappoint you. I need to let you know that before we embark on this acquaintance."

Micha realized that she was probably still in mourning. "I understand," he said. "This town is full of old people with whom I don't have much in common. I will enjoy a change of pace, too, and having someone to walk and talk with will brighten my days."

They started seeing each other. Their time together was sweet and gentle. Micha's presence in Lena's life helped her heal and regain some of her youthful joy. However, her heart was not yet free to be given to another.

Micha was a serious person. In his thirties he had graduated from a university in Milan, where he earned a degree in geology.

He had a keen mind and a thirst for knowledge. He lived with two unmarried sisters, Gita and Lila, in their parents' home. His oldest sister, Sonia, was among the first wave of Latvian Jewish youth to immigrate to Palestine and establish a new life in Tel Aviv. Micha didn't share his sister's passion for a revival of a Jewish land. He hoped to settle into a quiet life and start his own family. His need for fun and celebration did not match Lena's natural disposition, before she was grief stricken by the loss of Ilia, but his kind, generous manner did capture her interest.

The couple kept each other company. Lena enjoyed their walks and discussions of world affairs and the future of their people. It felt good to have someone to ease her loneliness. Micha was aware of Lena's reservations about their relationship and agreed to keep it low key.

A year went by. The couple strolled in one of the city's beautiful parks. Autumn made its presence felt and winter was not far behind. A light breeze engulfed them in a whirl of golden leaves. Lena picked up a bright yellow leaf, fallen off an elm tree, and studied it closely. "It's beautiful isn't it," she said, "the way nature keeps performing its duties with no concern about how sad our lives can turn."

"She is still thinking about her losses," thought Micha. "I wonder if she has any feelings for me." He stopped and turned her to face him. Lena raised her eyes in question. "I love you Lena," he said, "and I would like you to be my wife. Life goes on, you know, and, at some point, we need to create new choices and make plans for our futures. I know I am not everything you dreamed of in a husband, but this is all I can offer you. Please take your time and think how you want to answer me. If we are not to be together, I am planning to leave this little town and go start a life in another place. Probably Riga, where I will be able to find employment in my field."

Somewhat surprised, Lena reached for his hand. She raised it to her lips and kissed it lightly. "You are a wonderful, kind person," she said. "I feel lucky to have met you. Let me think about what you said. I promise to consider it and give you my answer."

Word of Micha's proposal spread throughout the community. All those close to Moshe's family were shaking their heads and wagging their tongues. "He is such a good *shidduch* (match) for Lena. How could she refuse that? She is no spring chicken, and there aren't that many eligible young men in town." Lena was approaching her mid-twenties, not quite an old maid but getting close, according to Jewish tradition. It was true that few exciting marriage prospects remained in their town. Many of the people her age had left, headed to a new country, excited to start a new life. Those who didn't share Lena's passions and aspirations were of little interest to her.

Feeling lost for answers and under family and social pressure, Lena accepted Micha's proposal. She was aware of her father's age and his lack of enthusiasm and energy for the family business since the death of his wife. She figured that the upkeep of the house and the shop would benefit from additional strong, young hands.

Micha did not become the love of her life, but, with his sweet generous nature, he gained her respect and affection.

They were married in the winter of 1940. A year later Lena gave birth to a baby girl. She was named after her grandmother, Nechama, Ama for short.

Micha moved into the family home. Lena continued taking care of her father and younger brother, Ilka. Micha joined Moshe in the fabric store, and life settled into a comfortable routine. Lena didn't regain her joyous spirit. Her baby daughter filled some of the void caused by the many losses she had experienced at such a young age.

9

Europe was sizzling with hatred toward the Jews

The future became uncertain. Europe was sizzling with hatred towards the Jews. In November 1938, a series of violent anti-Jewish attacks, known as Kristallnacht, took place in Germany, Austria, and Czechoslovakia. The violence was incited by the Nazi party. More than 75,000 Jewish-owned businesses were destroyed, and 267 synagogues burned. Close to 100 Jews were murdered, while 30,000 Jewish men were arrested and sent to concentration camps, their homes and assets confiscated by the German authorities.

The second World War was launched on September 1, 1939, with Germany's invasion of Poland. Soon after, the progress of the German army towards northeastern Europe began.

The Baltic States were annexed by Russia in June 1940. A vast number of the Latvian population was deported as free labor into sparsely inhabited areas of the Soviet Union. Many of them died in exile from starvation and poor living conditions.

A year later, when the German army was approaching the borders of the Baltic States, the population saw them as liberators from the Soviet occupation. By the end of June 1941, this fantasy was dispelled. Latvia became a part of Nazi Germany. Instead of liberation, anyone who disobeyed was killed or sent to a concentration camp.

Rumors were reaching the Jewish population. What they heard was difficult to apprehend as truth. According to eyewitnesses fleeing north from Poland, a systematic annihilation of Jews was taking place. Businesses and homes were confiscated and whole families relocated to ghettos or concentration camps.

The young and able were not about to stay behind and find out if these rumors were true. They fled in droves.

Moshe urged his daughter and son-in-law to take their newborn infant and flee east into the vastness of Russia where it was easy to lose oneself.

Ilka, Lena's younger brother, 19 at the time, was planning to ride his bicycle to the Russian border to reach the first town with a railroad system. He pleaded with his father before departing. "Come, Papa. Come with us. I can give you a ride on my bicycle."

Moshe, sad and tired, replied: "You children are young. You need to get away to safety. I am an old man. No one will harm me. I am no threat to anyone. You go and create a life where you'll be safe. We shall meet again, here in our home, when it's safe to return."

He reached out his arms and picked up his infant granddaughter, who had his beloved wife's name. Four-month-old Ama had a serious expression on her little face, as if she sensed the gravity of the situation. Her green eyes darted back to her mother, in whose arms, she instinctively felt, was the safest place for her. Moshe loved his little granddaughter. She brought a ray of sunshine to his sad life. The thought of losing her depressed him. In his mid-fifties, Moshe felt old, as if the winter of his days was approaching fast.

10

The earth seemed abandoned

The flat wooden cart was hitched to two tired-looking horses. The group of people, clutching their meager belongings, was nearly too much for the poor beasts to pull. The farmer providing this ride for a hefty price was determined to reach the Russian border, where he was to deposit his passengers.

The summer breeze felt warm on the faces of the travelers. The weather in this part of the world rarely showed extremes. Summers were mild. Golden fields ready to be harvested greeted the travelers. The wheat stalks were bending with the weight of the grain. There were no workers in the fields. All able-bodied men had been drafted. The earth seemed abandoned. There was a threatening stillness in the air. The silence was ominous. It felt like a calm before a great storm. The storm was approaching from the west.

The Baltic States were the gateway for German advancement into Russia. This was the beginning of the deadliest war in history, a war that dragged on for six years, involving more than 30 countries.

Lena and Micha, with four-month-old Ama, were perched on the platform, legs dangling off the edge. Their only belongings were two leather suitcases and a cloth sack with Ama's diapers. Lena's brother, Ilka, peddled on his bicycle, keeping pace with the carriage. Lena clutched her daughter to her chest. Her blue eyes were staring without seeing. She was getting further and further away from the only home she had known since her birth. Her father's lonely image, standing on the side of the road, waving as they departed, was imprinted on her mind. She had become his main emotional and physical support after her mother's death.

Moshe insisted they all take a moment and sit down on their luggage before departing and heading towards an unknown future. Sitting on the packed suitcases before a long journey was an old ingrained Russian custom, done in silence and contemplation. It was about calming down, collecting one's thoughts, and making sure you have everything you might need on your trip.

Lena struggled with contradictory emotions of guilt for leaving her father alone, relief for escaping in time, and apprehension of what lay ahead.

Running alongside the carriage were the unlucky ones, those who hadn't found means of transportation. They were hoping to find a spot on the moving platform, a space they could hop onto.

Among them was a young woman with a baby in her arms, running alongside the carriage. She spotted Lena sitting on the edge of the platform. "Please," the woman cried, "take my baby with you. Save my baby." Lena, clutching her own baby to her breast, averted her eyes from the woman, a lone teardrop trailing down her cheek.

11

Away from the approaching hooves of German horses

After a 63-kilometer journey to the Russian border riding on a wooden plank, Lena and Micha felt beyond exhaustion. Little Ama protested the bumpy ride with inconsolable crying and clenched fists. Lena clutched Ama to her chest, trying to calm her down, to no avail. The main elements a four-month-old baby needs—timely meals and a peaceful environment—were gone. She had to get accustomed to a new existence in which food and rest were not given commodities. Lena kept looking back, making sure she could see Ilka trailing them on his bicycle.

The group stopped along the side of the road to allow the passengers to relieve themselves and stretch their limbs. Lena and Micha, joined by Ilka, spread a clean cloth on the ground underneath a grove of Aspen trees and shared the food they had brought from home. The leaves made a glorious golden canopy high above them. Nature was oblivious to human tragedy. The mood was somber. Each one of them was trapped in his own thoughts.

"Do you think Papa will be all right?" asked Lena.

"My sisters will be able to help him if he is in need," answered Micha. Lena rolled her eyes. Her sisters-in-law, who remained spinsters, did not possess their brother's sweet nature. At the ripe old age of 34, he was considered beyond marrying age, and his sisters had secretly hoped that he'd remain a bachelor and continue taking care of their needs. Marrying Lena did not bring them joy, and they made it clear to her.

The next stop was a small town near the Russian border. This was as far as the carriage was taking them. From here they had to find their own means to get to Moscow, where they were planning to board a train, heading away from the border, away from the approaching hooves of German horses.

The prevailing notion was that heading south to the Mediterranean region of Asia was a sound idea. For those who had recently been displaced from their homes, the weather in the southern region, compared to the approaching Russian fall and winter, offered the promise of survival.

The Russian railway system was the main mode of transportation; it connected the major cities. If your destination was a distant part of the country through less populated regions, the means of transportation were by carriage or on foot.

Moscow's train station swarmed with people rushing all around them. The big-city atmosphere overwhelmed the travelers. They had grown up in a small town. Lena felt dizzy. She clutched the baby under her coat. It was a black sealskin coat that her father had given to her before they embarked on their journey. The weather did not warrant such heavy protection. Her fear of losing the little she had brought with her from home made her carry whatever possible on her body.

The train station was packed with those who, overnight, had lost their homes, their livelihoods, and a predictable way of life. Many had left parents, brothers, and sisters. Their pasts were left behind with no knowledge of what lurked in their futures.

Ama's little digestive system was touchy. The cloth sack, which had been packed with fresh diapers and guarded with utmost care by Lena, was now packed with soiled ones. She was hoping to come by a river on their travels, where she planned to wash the diapers. In the confusion of a moment, while Lena turned away from her belongings, the sack containing the diapers was snatched by some seedy vagrant. The loss was grave. Lena's sweet revenge was imagining the culprit opening his loot and finding the stolen treasure.

12

I have a baby and we are hungry

The road to safety was challenging. The means of transportation to the various destinations in such a vast country were unpredictable. Refugees were trying to escape as far away from the advancing Germans as possible. The train cars zoomed by, filled beyond capacity.

The train they boarded took them on a long, slow ride with frequent stops along its route. It was packed with people fleeing their homes. Rucksacks, suitcases, and cardboard boxes tied with rope were strewn across the aisles, obstructing movement. The country was on the move. An unknown future created an atmosphere of fear and mistrust.

Lena was dozing off, lulled by the rhythm of the train with a sleeping Ama in her arms. Micha kept a watchful eye on their belongings, and Ilka was huddled in the corner of a bench catching some much-needed sleep. The train came to a sudden halt. Through the window Lena noticed a line of soldiers waiting by a shed. They were standing patiently, waiting for their turn to approach a small window through which a uniformed person handed them each a loaf of bread. The rationed bread was served only to those in uniform.

The food Lena and her family had packed for their travels was running low. Lena jumped off her seat and dropped the baby into Micha's unprepared arms. She hastily shared with him her plan. "You are crazy," blurted Micha. "These rations are given only to soldiers. They will chase you away."

"We shall see," hissed Lena. "We have hardly any food left and the way to our next destination is still long. I must try. Hold on to the baby. Make sure she is covered and warm." Micha didn't have a chance to argue with his wife. He remained seated, a squirming Ama in his arms. Caring for the baby was not his strong point. He was a book person, quite useless at childcare. His skills had not prepared him for the curves life was throwing at him.

He watched Lena through the train's window, hesitantly approaching the line of soldiers. She was a small woman and looked forlorn trailing behind the tall young man who was the last in line for the bread rations. The line moved slowly. The train was nearing its departure time. "All aboard," announced a voice through the loudspeaker. The conductor was calling all to return to the train. Micha felt the sweat running down along the side of his face. He was facing the threat of losing his wife and being left alone with an infant to care for. The thought filled him with dread.

The last soldier with his loaf of bread boarded the train. Lena approached the window, looked into the supply clerk's face and blurted her story with one line: "I have a baby and we are hungry."

The train started its departure. Micha knew that all was lost. He and his wife would, most likely, not be able to reunite. The country was vast. It was easy to lose one another. "I will get off at the next stop and go back to look for her," said Ilka, trying to reassure his brother-in-law. "I will find her. You make sure the baby stays safe," he added, taking Ama out of Micha's shaky arms.

Lena, clutching a loaf of bread to her breast, ran alongside the moving train. She managed to grab hold of the last car's rail and hoist herself up onto the train's step. The doors were locked. She rode the whole way to the next town standing on the train's step, holding on to the loaf of bread with one arm and the train's rail with the other, waiting for the train to stop. When it did, she found her way back to where Micha, Ilka, and the baby were lamenting her loss.

When Micha laid eyes on his wife, he could hardly contain his fury. The meager loaf of bread she had gained was no consolation for the terror he felt when he believed he had lost her and was left alone with Ama.

13

The fresh milk streamed into the vessel

There were rumors that the German invasion of the Soviet Union had begun. Operation Barbarossa was the largest and the most powerful invasion force in human history. The Baltic States were the gateway to Russia's eastern borders and the first to be invaded. The German army was advancing towards Leningrad.

The train stations were mobbed with displaced people, huddled in the corners, nodding off, holding on to their belongings, waiting to be taken away, far away. The greater the distance Lena and her family could reach, the greater was their hope of survival.

Lena, Micha, Ilka, and little Ama continued their way to the south. They hoped to reach the southern states of Russia, a place with warmer weather. They traveled by foot when no other transportation was available. At local markets along their travels, they purchased food and supplies, exchanging money and jewelry they brought with them from home.

The Russian autumn was already biting at their heels. They were homeless, counting on the hospitality of farm owners encountered along their travels to allow them to spend the chilly nights in their drafty barns.

Ama, barely five months old, was carried in a makeshift pack on Lena's back, their belongings carried by the man and the boy. The long treks and the weight of the luggage forced them to stop and rest often. The miles they covered daily amounted to slow progress.

The fall season was glorious. Nature was not taking sides on this war-torn continent. The fields were lush green. The trees, turning to gold and fiery red, greeted them along the way. Small quaint farms with spans of orchards waiting to be harvested were nestled in the fields. They didn't stop to enjoy the idyllic scenes they passed. Their circumstances didn't allow it.

Food was running low. Ama was not content. Her constant crying was heart wrenching. She was hungry. Lena's inability to replenish her own food was a hindrance. Her milk was not abundant.

They reached a grove of trees and settled down to rest. The trees graced them with a cool, reviving umbrella of shade. The grasses around them were tall and supple. Near where they settled, they noticed, sharing their shade, two hefty cows, grazing on the luscious grass. The animals eyed the newcomers with curiosity but no evident hostility.

Ilka had a mischievous smile spreading on his young face. He motioned to the others to be quiet. With a cup in his hand, he inched gently towards the cows and started stroking one of them with a gentle hand. Soon enough he made a friend. The creature was nuzzling his face with her wet snout in obvious delight. With one hand holding the cup under her belly he started squeezing her utter. The fresh milk streamed into the vessel. The day was saved. Ama had her first taste of rich, nourishing raw cow's milk.

14

God seemed to have abandoned them

Lena and Micha were roaming through the farmer's market of Rostov, a small settlement along the Volga. They stopped at an inn to rest, regroup, buy food and supplies, preparing to continue their journey towards the south.

The market was buzzing with merchants and patrons eager to snatch the meager supply of fresh fruits and vegetables offered. Ama was perched on her mother's right hip and held in the crook of her right arm. She watched the colorful crowds of people with fascination, holding on tight to her mother's arm. Lena was rummaging through the merchandise while keeping a close watch on the leather handbag with its strap hanging off her left shoulder. Her pragmatic nature caused her lack of trust.

Micha, the eternal scholar, was fascinated by the stalls offering a variety of books for sale. The price was low, and he was mesmerized by the many subjects offered. Lena, finding him immersed in the books, bristled. "We are not spending the few *kopeks (Russian coins)* we have on books," she hissed.

"But they are so cheap," he pleaded. Between the two of them, she was the practical one. The responsibility of ensuring they had enough food to sustain them quickly became hers.

A commotion behind them caught their attention. People were pushing and shoving. Some were swearing and yelling at each other. A fistfight broke out, and all attention was focused on the two struggling figures. Soon spirits quieted down. All returned their attention to the business of commerce.

With a shriek of anger Lena realized that her leather handbag was gone. The staged commotion was enacted for the sole purpose of distracting her and those around her, enabling the thieves to cut the handles with a razor and get away with the purse she had slung on her shoulder. It was gone, with their money and a few mementos she carried from home.

Lena fell to her knees and sobbed inconsolably to a God that, at that moment, seemed to have abandoned them.

15

He took care of more than just the farm's equipment

One morning they woke up in a barn. They had arrived the night before, tired, and hungry. It was late. The sun was disappearing fast. A chill descended over the travelers. They had to find refuge for the night before dark. They approached a small farmhouse nestled along a winding road.

A middle-aged woman stood at the gate, eying them with curiosity and some suspicion. She and her daughter were alone. The men had been drafted in June, at the start of the invasion.

Ilka, the smooth talker, walked towards her, offering his hand and a big disarming smile in greeting. "Hello," he'd said, bowing his head in a gesture of respect. "We are traveling south, we are coming all the way from Riga, escaping the advancing German army."

The woman considered his words carefully. Her eyes traveled from him to the young mother holding a baby. The sight of the woman cradling a tiny baby in her arms had touched her. She felt compassion for the tired mother. "If you'd be so kind as to let us spend the night in your barn," continued Ilka, noticing the shift in her emotions, "I'll help you with some of your chores around the farm."

The woman stared at him, considering his offer, and asked, "Can you fix broken equipment? The men of this household are fighting at the front. My daughter and I are alone, taking care of the farm. Some of our equipment is in immediate need of repair or we will not be able to plow and harvest."

"I am a master of repair," responded Ilka enthusiastically.

The next day, his able hands fixed the farm's malfunctioning equipment, to the delight of the farmer's wife and the admiration of her daughter who, by then, had managed to change her dress to a more revealing one and undo her braids to reveal a lush curly mane the color of the sun. She was smiling at Ilka with adoring eyes. "Indeed, he is a handsome lad," she thought.

The second night, Ilka's family was invited to a hot meal in the farmer's modest kitchen. Over potato soup and braised cabbage, they shared stories of a glorious past and hopes for a safe and peaceful future. The vodka poured and spirits sored. Human friendship prevailed. For one night, the horrors of war were left behind.

That night, Lena and Micha, with little Ama, were again nestled comfortably in the barn with proper blankets given to them by the farmer's wife. Ilka did not share their place of rest that night. The contented smile on the farmer's daughter's face the next morning attested to the fact that he took care of more than just the farm's equipment.

16

I need to go back and join the fighting troops

They were three months into their journey. Their progress was painfully slow. Ama was a contented baby, as long as she could rely on enough food to satisfy her constant hunger. Lena's milk was sparse. The adults became malnourished. Micha was a retiring, gentle soul without much resourcefulness to try and improve their conditions. Ilka kept milking stray cows along the way to help feed little Ama, but his young, active spirit was becoming restless.

Traveling refugees they encountered on their way brought news of the war. Massive numbers of German troops were approaching Moscow. Stalin directed a scorching defense.

Ilka, approaching his twentieth birthday, became somber and moody. Being a young, able-bodied man, he felt the urge to take part in the fighting that was engulfing the continent. The slow travel to safety with his sister and her family seemed less important. He yearned to join the fighting at the front. Lena, knowing her brother's restless spirit, had been afraid that this day would come.

"I love you all," said Ilka, "but I must leave you. You have each other and you will be fine once you reach a place of safety. I need to go back and join the fighting troops."

He lifted little Ama high in the air and swung her around to the sound of her giggles. He kissed her on both cheeks and touched his forehead to hers. "I need to leave you, *mayo sol-nyshkuh*" *(my sunshine)*, he whispered, "but I promise to come and visit you very soon." Ama moved her face close to his and kissed him on the lips. Her face lit up with a big smile. Her uncle was playing a game with her, she thought.

Ilka hugged Micha and embraced his sister. She held onto him for a long time, as if to keep him safe forever in the shelter of her arms. They said their goodbyes with heavy hearts. Lena remained standing in one place for a long while, shading her eyes against the sun, trailing his disappearing image into the distance. They parted ways, not knowing if they'd ever see each other again.

17

The horses' hooves hit a soft surface

Tashkent, the capital of Uzbekistan, is a large city, known for its cotton growing, natural resources, and some industry. It is also blessed with long summers and mild winters. Their hope was to find employment and a modest place to live to wait out the war in safety.

Syr Darya is a river along the northeast side of Uzbekistan. Lena and Micha had to cross it to reach their destination. The long train ride deposited them in Symkent, 300 kilometers north of the river's shores. They continued their journey with hired carriages pulled by horses. The journey took ten days.

It was the last stretch of their travels towards their destination. They saw the grand river glistening in the distance. They had to decide whether to cross the river before nightfall or seek shelter for the night and cross the river the next day.

The coachman they hired was a veteran of winters in these parts. For a hefty sum, he offered to take them further, across the river. The surface of the water seemed frozen. They trusted him to know when it was safe to cross. "I don't think the river's surface is safe to travel on," whispered Micha to Lena. He was the cautious one.

"He would know if it were not," responded Lena, who was the adventurous one. "I don't want to stay another night in a flea-ridden rented room. Let's just get on with it and arrive at our destination. We are so close. The sooner we can start sleeping in our own beds, the better."

They huddled in the back of the carriage. Lena did prevail but with a sense of apprehension. The coachman urged the horses to hasten their pace across the river, as if a hurried pace ensured a safer passage. The distance seemed to stretch forever. Around them they could hear the crackle of ice. It was not in its most solid state. They were a month early.

As they approached the shore, the horses' hooves hit a soft surface. The beasts' legs started to disappear into the ice. Water reached the carriage minutes after its passengers managed to jump out. Micha held Ama high above the freezing water, while Lena salvaged their luggage from the sinking carriage. They were close to the riverbank. Trudging to shore, they fell into the helping arms of bystanders, who had watched the drama unfold.

They were offered dry clothes and a place to stay for the night. The generosity of those that welcomed them touched their hearts and brought hope for the future. Their first experience in the place that was to become their home combined both fear and gratitude.

Lena, in later years, shared this story with Ama often. She would describe the close call they experienced with the sinking carriage. Ama liked listening to her mother's stories. She had questions and wanted to know details. "What happened to the horses?" she kept asking. "Mama, did the horses drown?" The fate of the animals was a big concern to her. Lena would look at her with astonished blue eyes that offered no answers. Empathy for any life form other than their own hadn't crossed her mind.

18

It felt like discovering a vein of gold

The one room Micha and Lena could afford became their safe haven. No more begging for a stay in the corner of a drafty barn. They were safe from persecution. There was no need to look behind their backs, no need to be afraid of being hunted.

Ama took her first steps. She was a slender baby. Walking came easily to her, and she was determined. One day she looked up at her mother with thoughtful eyes and struggled to speak. Lena scooped her up and tried to coax her into expressing her first word. "M...M...Mama," Lena helped her along, convinced that this was the word Ama was trying to learn. Ama shook her head vigorously to signal a "no."

"*Chleb*," uttered Ama, to Lena's surprise. The first word Ama struggled to master was a request for bread.

Micha was a patient, loving father. He reveled in his daughter's keen mind and interest in everything that surrounded her. He taught her how to look at flowers and butterflies and explained why the two sought each other's company. He took her on long walks in the countryside, pointing out blossoming trees and explaining why there were so many bees swarming around. He was the one expanding her mind. Lena was the practical parent, making sure that all their physical needs were met. They were a good match for raising a balanced, emotionally and physically nurtured child.

In their tiny kitchen Lena prepared their meals. Food was scarce and not always fresh, consisting mainly of grain and potatoes.

On her visits to the local market Lena befriended a farmer. He took a liking to the young woman walking through the stalls, a baby on her hip, trying to discern what produce she could afford. On one of those outings, he called her over and placed a paper bag with corn seeds in her hand. "These seeds will sustain you and your family through the winter," he told Lena. "I will teach you how to sow the seeds and when to harvest the ripe corn." He proceeded to instruct her on how to grow her own corn.

The warm weather was just right. Her little plot at the outskirts of town bore its crop three months later. Lena walked among the tall and supple stalks. The ears turned dark green, the silk turned brown, and the kernels were soft and plump. Lena, holding an ear of corn in her hands, one she grew herself, was filled with wonder. It felt like discovering a vein of gold.

She followed the farmer's instructions, tied the ears of the corn in bundles and hung them upside down to dry in a corner of their tiny kitchen.

Her trek to the nearest mill was long. The sack on her back was heavy, but her sense of triumph made the weight insignificant.

The smaller sack of coarse corn flour she carried back home sustained them for months to come.

19

The boots were a reddish-brown shade

Uzbekistan was one of the central Asian states that became a haven to 1.1 million refugees from the German-occupied territories. Many of them were Jews. They were the lucky ones, escaping their homelands before the German troops marched into their towns and villages. Out of over a million people left behind, 300,000 perished from disease or starvation, languishing in ghettos, or dying in their flight to find refuge.

Tashkent, the capital of Uzbekistan, was home to many colorful cultures, primarily Muslim. Several languages were spoken in the streets, dominated by Arabic, Persian, and Russian. The Moorish architecture graced the town with mosques from whose towers the muezzin called the faithful to their daily prayers.

Chorsu, Tashkent's old town, had one of the busiest markets. Women of all ages were selling food, household items and knickknacks, hoping to make a profit to support their families. Other stalls offered colorful textiles and crafts. Vendors enticed passersby with their colorful goods.

Lena strolled among the many stalls, carrying Ama on her hip. She eyed the beautiful clothing, knowing she was in no position to spend the little money they had. A pair of child's felt boots caught her eye. Ama was just starting to take her first steps. She needed footwear. The boots were a reddish-brown shade, woven tightly from boiled wool.

Ama beamed with delight at the new boots on her feet. The added newspaper Lena stuffed inside the boots made them even safer against moisture.

20

Medicine was often diluted with water

The large local general store was owned by a Pakistani man named Akmal. He was an industrious business owner, determined to supply the people in his neighborhood with all their possible necessities. A small corner of his store was designated as the local pharmacy.

The medicines dispensed by pharmacies were closely monitored by the authorities. Supplying people with their medications was not always done aboveboard. Medicine was often diluted with water or crushed sugar, a practice Akmal took advantage of.

Micha, in his search for employment, approached the owner of the store. Akmal liked the young man's honest face. He needed an accomplice he could trust. Micha didn't like the idea of defrauding those in need of medicine. After giving Akmal's proposal some thought, he decided he had to compromise his integrity. He was put to work in the pharmacy.

The work was steady, and so was Micha's pay. They settled into a comfortable, predictable life. Lena stayed home and cared for their daughter. She was able to help with their living expenses by caring for a neighbor's child whose parents were employed during the day. Micha was busy dispensing medicines to the neighborhood patrons, under Akmal's watchful eye.

21

If you are caught, you'll be sent to prison

One morning they awoke to loud knocking on their front door. They had no friends or family nearby. The banging on the door was persistent and sounded ominous.

"Micha Cherfas?" A soldier in Russian uniform faced Micha at the open door. "You are hereby ordered to report for duty. You are to join a military base, stationed near Moscow. You have two days to get your affairs in order." Micha, being a Latvian citizen, was enlisted in the Latvian troops.

As a young male, not being in uniform, he had roused the suspicions of their neighbors. Malicious tongues informed on him to the authorities, and he was quickly assigned to a fighting troop near Moscow.

Micha's employment at the pharmacy was a desirable position. He convinced Akmal to employ Lena after his departure. "She is smart and a fast learner," he told Akmal. "She also understands and follows what needs to be done," he added, with a covert look that only the two of them understood.

"There are some things I need to tell you," he confided to Lena as he was getting ready for his departure. "Not all sales of medicines at Akmal's pharmacy are aboveboard. I had to go along with his instructions whether I liked it or not. He will ask you to do the same. Remember, it is dangerous. If you are caught by the authorities, you'll be sent to a Siberian prison. I know you, and I know your spirit of adventure. Follow his instructions, but do not overdo it. Don't do anything stupid. That will ruin us all."

The next morning, with a few belongings packed in a small backpack, Micha was ready to depart. He picked up his little daughter, nuzzled her face and said, "Amichka, *ya dolzhen uyti.*" *(I have to go away.)* "You are a big girl now. Take care of your mama until I come back, which will be very soon."

Ama stared at him skeptically. She remembered her Uncle Ilka leaving and considered the fact that he wasn't in her life anymore. She shook her head vigorously. "I don't want you to go," she said, trying hard not to cry. She held his face in her two little hands and pressed her wet cheek against his. Micha handed his daughter to his wife, embraced them both and quickly departed.

Ama watched her father's figure grow smaller, descending the winding road. It was a cool autumn morning. Grey clouds gathered across the sky. This would always remind Ama of departures and the loss of loved ones.

Ama's happy, quiet life changed overnight. A kind, elderly neighbor agreed to take on her daily care while Lena worked at Akmal's pharmacy. She was a quick learner and was able to expertly follow his instructions on how to deceive the customers.

The Russian army was in distress. Any male, young or not so young, able enough to fight, was drafted. The Latvian army, where Micha was sent, was small and untrained. They were mainly used as the first wave on the battleground to slow down the progress of the approaching German forces. Micha was assigned to a Latvian armor division.

22

Above his head, a lone white dove was flying in large circles

Lena exited their little apartment into the sunlit street. She had just left Ama with the elderly woman who watched her when she was at work. She hurried to get to the pharmacy in time for its opening. Ama watched her mother go with concern. Her daughter's distressed little face haunted Lena. She knew that Ama was anxious when left behind, fearful that those she loved and counted on for her survival would not return.

Lena noticed a man in uniform approaching her with a hasty pace. His face was grim but determined. Above his head, a lone white dove was flying in large circles.

She felt her heart constrict and hastened her pace. He stopped her and handed her an official envelope. It had the stamp of the Russian army across its front. She realized instantly the news it might carry.

A strangled sob pierced the silence and Lena realized that it had come from deep inside her. She took the letter from his extended hand, opened it, and read the first line. "We regret to inform you . . ." The letter fell to the ground and tumbled in the breeze along the dirt road, as rejected and unwanted as the news it carried.

Micha had been sent to battle without any training. His tank and its crew were destroyed two weeks after his enlistment. Lena became a widow at the age of 28. Ama lost her father when she was two-and-a-half years old.

23

Summer was approaching and with it, kinder weather

Lena was lonely. There was no one to share her life or fall back on in times of need. The small apartment she had shared with Micha, the haven they had created for their little family, became a sad place where she was just existing, and waiting, wondering about her father's fate and whether her younger brother, Ilka, was surviving the bloody war. She and Ilka shared the gene for courage and adventure. She knew he wasn't one to sit through the war in a safe post. She knew he would choose to be in an active war zone. She worried about him the most. It became nerve wracking, waiting for news that trickled sporadically from the front. She missed her family and her friends.

Summer was approaching and, with it, kinder weather. Lena started to plan the next chapter of their lives.

Rumors reached them. Germany's advancement into Eastern Europe and Russia encountered fierce resistance. The battle of Stalingrad was the first significant German loss and a turning point of World War II. The Soviet army started to push the German troops back.

A new hope seeped into people's hearts. They hoped that an end to this ferocious war, an end to their nightmare, might become a reality.

The main battle grounds moved to the western borders. The central part of Russia became relatively safe for travel. Lena dug out a letter given to her by her father, Moshe, as they were leaving their home, escaping into Russia. "Keep this letter," he had said, looking urgently into her eyes. "It contains names and contact information of family members scattered throughout Russia. My hope is to see you all back here at home with me very soon, but you never know. It might prove useful."

Lena's plan was to head north towards Siberia. Her father's letter mentioned distant cousins living in the Ural Mountains region in a town named Ufa, the capital of Bashkiria.

The Ural Mountains extend along the eastern border of Russia. The war had not reached that part of the country. Life in the north, although affected by the war in every other way, was not in danger of occupation.

Lena pulled out the old, trusted leather suitcase and backpack they had arrived with two years ago and got ready for their trip.

24

Out of his pocket he pulled a candy

Fifteen hundred miles on the road turned into a long adventure laced with difficult challenges. Lena, at the age of 28, alone with a three-year-old toddler, was venturing on a trip that would have been difficult in peacetime and was especially challenging in times of war.

The railway system played a vital role in the war effort, transporting military personnel, equipment, and freight to the front lines, as well as evacuating factories, and entire towns, away from the embattled war zones to the Ural and Siberian regions.

Lena was determined to reach a place where she might find family members and settle again into a life of safety for her and her daughter.

The train stations were in mayhem. Soldiers heading to their units were given priority in boarding. People fleeing from battle zones, their belongings on their backs, were struggling to board a train, find a corner, sitting or standing, eager to stretch the distance between them and the destruction of war.

Trains zoomed by without stopping, packed to their limit with passengers, leaving no space for additional travelers. Huddled along the station's walls were tired, displaced people, waiting for a train that would stop and allow them to board.

Lena, exhausted, sat heavily on a wooden bench at the corner of the station, away from huddled groups of people. She handed Ama a corn cake she had packed before they left Tashkent. The next train wasn't due until the next morning. She had to share the long night with groups of strangers, all caught up in the same predicament.

An elderly man approached her and Ama. He bent down and tousled the child's hair. Out of his pocket he pulled a candy in a colorful wrapper and handed it to Ama, who looked up at her mother for approval and only then reached and took the candy. Lena smiled at the stranger and whispered: "*Spasiba*" *(Thank you)*. She gazed after his retreating figure and sighed, feeling a bit more hopeful, more relaxed. She laid Ama across her knees, covered her with her coat, leaned her head back, and slept.

25

Lena, I am here—Ilka

The town of Orsk marked half the distance Lena and Ama had to travel to reach their destination, the town of Ufa.

The train neared the town's borders. The vast wheat fields this area was known for were barren and neglected. Farm workers were scarce. The women could not shoulder the heavy agricultural effort needed to sustain the growing and harvesting of crops. In the distance, Lena could see the smokestacks of Orsk's refineries. The skies were a mix of smoke and grey, signaling the approaching winter. Lena was anxious to reach Ufa before the bitter Russian cold landed on them.

Orsk's station platform swarmed with people getting off the train, heading to different destinations. A few scattered travelers were left on the platform. Like Lena, they were considering their next move.

Her attention was drawn to a wall in the back of the station. In black chalk she noticed large letters. Her eyes opened in astonishment. The letters read, "Lena, I am here, Ilka." The message from her brother was clear. He had learned about her travels and had thought of an ingenious way to try and connect with her. Train stations were a sound possibility to find each other.

"Well, I'll be damned," whispered Lena. "He is here. Ilka is here. I have to find him." She grabbed their belonging and

Ama's hand and rushed into town in search of a refugee center to inquire about a tall, handsome soldier named Ilka.

Orsk is one of the largest cities in western Russia. Searching such a place with no address was difficult. Ama was beyond exhaustion from the train ride and the frantic search through the city's streets. Perched on Lena's arm, her head resting on her mother's shoulder, she fell fast asleep.

"Are you lost?" came a question from behind Lena. She turned around and saw a young man approaching her with a long stride. He had a worried look on his face. The young woman carrying a suitcase in one hand, a backpack on her back and a sleeping toddler in her arms had concerned him.

"I am looking for a displaced-persons center," she said, placing the suitcase on the ground and wiping the perspiration from her brow. "I was told there is one in town?"

"Let me take you there," he said. Picking up her suitcase, he motioned her to follow him. They walked side by side, passing long blocks of a city in ruins. "It is heartbreaking to see this town so destroyed by the war," he muttered.

"Where are you from?" asked Lena.

"I was born here," he answered, "this is my home. It used to be a beautiful town. Look at it now. War is a terrible thing," he added. They continued walking in silence. "The center is a couple of blocks from here," said the young man.

"You are very kind," said Lena, with sincere appreciation. They parted in front of the building's steps with a handshake. Ama, who was awake by now, eyed the young man with curiosity. He touched her cheek with a smile, *"Dasvidaniya malenkiy"* (*Goodby little one*), he said, and walked off.

The center helped people find out the whereabouts of loved ones. It was situated in the middle of town. Large groups were gathered on the front steps, waiting for any news that might reunite them with their families. They were immersed in lively conversations, sharing their travel experiences and their future plans.

Lena walked in the front door, squeezing through a group that huddled expectantly in the doorway. There was no way to know how old her brother's message was—days, weeks, months? She was excited by the thought of meeting him but tried not to be too hopeful. She entered the main office. The man behind the counter directed her to a large hall in the center of the building. Groups of soldiers were exchanging news about the progress of the war and information about the safety of traveling.

Ilka saw her first as she hesitantly entered the room with Ama clutched to her neck. He limped towards her, leaning on his cane. He had been wounded in his leg and was now on leave to let his wounds heal.

Lena's eyes fell on the young man in uniform, slowly approaching her with a broad, joyous smile. She responded with a strangled sound, half a sob of relief and half a cry of joy. She grabbed her younger brother with her free arm and held on to him in a tight embrace shaken by her sobs, which spoke of the lonely days and nights of her last few months.

"*Amichka dorogaya*" *(dear)*, said Ilka, reaching for Ama with his free arm. "Look at how you have grown!" Ama stared at the familiar face, frowning. The voice carried memories of the past. The image of the soldier reaching out to her did not. Ama shrugged and hid her face against Lena's shoulder.

Ilka had learned about Micha's death and his sister's decision to travel into central and northern Russia when his search for her in Tashkent bore no result

They walked arm in arm to a nearby bench. Ama, holding on to her mother's coattails, trailed along. The feeling of being held and protected was like a healing balm to Lena. It had been over two years since Ilka enlisted, leaving Lena, Micha, and baby Ama standing on a deserted country road. They had been traveling south, searching for safety, while he was heading back north to join the fighting forces. He looked older. The experience of war was etched on his young face.

The Ural River runs along the outskirts of Orsk. They walked along its shore. Ilka didn't have any news about their father. They were both worried.

"When were you wounded?" asked Lena. "Is it a serious injury?"

"Just a scratch," answered Ilka. "It is practically healed." Lena eyed him skeptically. His limp and use of the cane indicated differently.

Ilka shared stories of his war experience, and Lena talked about months of loneliness and her decision to travel and look for relatives who might offer her and Ama companionship and safety. They reminisced about a sweet past and shared hopes for a brighter future.

Ama was mesmerized by this tall, handsome man who held her on his knees and showered her with attention and love. She vaguely remembered another man lifting her up to the sky and calling her name with affection. The memory of Micha was slowly fading away.

26

The first scar

Snow covered the ground. It was crisp and hard. The temperature plummeted below zero. The Russian winter was merciless. For the homeless, winter was the worst enemy.

Lena and Ama descended from the train at its last stop and started walking down a snow-covered road. The wet snowflakes landing lightly on their heads signaled the arrival of a heavy storm. They had to find shelter before dark and take a break from their travels, wait for it to pass.

The shack was tiny, part of a sprawling farmhouse. It was all that Lena could afford and it included a much-welcomed hot meal. The room offered one small cot and a wooden nightstand. The floor was bare; a naked light bulb was strung from the ceiling, casting a low, gloomy light on the room. They settled in for the night, sharing the cot. The shed's walls creaked with gusts of wind. Lena, exhausted by the long walk from the train station, embraced her daughter and fell into a deep sleep.

Ama couldn't sleep. Her head throbbed with pain. She whimpered and tossed her head from side to side. Lena, awakened from sleep, wrapped her little daughter in warm clothes and exited the shed. The winds died down. The storm had passed.

It was dark with only the light of the moon. They walked in the snow. Their footsteps left deep prints; their breath formed vapor in the air. The silence was disturbed only by the crunching of their boots. The pain in Ama's head slowly subsided. Lena was no stranger to aches and pains. She knew what to do. For Ama, this became a lifelong struggle. The pain in her head evolved into migraines.

Ama was a normal child who loved to play. She was often lost in an imaginary world, escaping the actual events of her life, a life that now included pain. The headaches became her frequent companions.

Early experiences of trauma can cause pain and emotional scaring, which can either make you weaker or stronger. It is said that physical scars are formed of fibers, not ordinary tissue, and that therefore they are stronger. Perhaps the same is true of emotional scars.

27

She goes where I go. My fate is hers

Anton and Irina were strolling through the farmer's market. It was their weekly shopping day.

Goods were scarce. Produce brought to market had little appeal or luster. The farms were poorly staffed. Most able-bodied men were at the front. War widows were shouldering the burden of caring for crops on their own. The news from the front blanketed all in a somber mood. The Germans were gaining ground.

Anton, as a worker in a munitions plant, was spared the draft. The young couple was making their way between the sparse vegetable stands when Irina noticed the fair-haired woman clutching a tiny toddler under her coat with one arm and carrying a tattered leather suitcase in the other. The little face with its tasseled fair hair peeking from under the woman's coat fascinated Irina. Something in the woman's bewildered gaze made Irina walk towards her and the child.

Irina and Anton had tried to have a baby during their ten years of marriage but could not conceive. Irina longed for the touch of sticky little hands around her neck. She longed for what this strange, lost woman clutched beneath her worn coat. Mesmerized, she approached the woman, gently touched her shoulder, and started a conversation. An hour later, Lena and Ama were sitting in Anton and Irina's apartment.

Ama's eyes grew wide. She had never seen such luxury. The floors were covered with beautiful rugs, and the furniture, though modest, was piled with thick, warm blankets to use on chilly evenings. Irina was fascinated by the lively toddler. Ama's vocabulary was developed, and she responded eagerly to the lavish attention she was getting. Irina had a beautiful, kind face, and Ama resigned herself to her hugs despite her reserved nature. Irina held Ama's hand and walked her to a waist-high niche recessed in the wall of the apartment. Irina padded it with soft blankets and pillows to create a small magical place for Ama to play in. The excitement and the warmth relaxed Ama, and, after a meal of sweet, soft porridge, she soon relaxed into a restful sleep.

Lena was seated at the table relishing the first hot, home-cooked meal she had experienced in many weeks.

"We are refugees," she shared. "My husband was killed. We are heading north to the Ural Mountains, to a town named Ufa, where I hope to connect with relatives and find a home for Ama and me."

There were tears in Irina's eyes. She could only imagine the long treacherous road this young woman still faced.

"You will never make it alive with this small child," she said. "For her sake, leave her with us. She will be safe and taken care of. She will have a good life. You are young. You have your whole life ahead of you. Not being burdened with a small child will give you a better chance of survival." There was longing in Irina's voice. Her eyes were pleading with Lena. She felt some hope. She wanted to adopt the little person sleeping in the cozy niche and hoped to convince the young woman that it was to her advantage to leave her child behind in their care.

Lena's eyes grew bright and fierce. "She goes where I go," she said. "My fate is hers."

After a restful night, Lena and Ama departed from their hosts with hugs and thanks and embarked on foot to the local train station.

28

She died during the night

Lena awoke in a panic. They spent the night in a small guest house not too far from the train station. Next to her, little Ama was burning up with fever. She had become lethargic the day before. Lena was watching her closely. She decided that a break from their travels to rest and let Ama recuperate would be wise. They still had a considerable distance to travel.

The fever did not break. Ama started shivering, her whole body glistening with sweat. Lena was terrified. She made the decision to head to the city's general hospital, an institution she didn't hold great trust in, especially in times of war when medical staff was scarce.

The conditions in a hospital during wartime were gloomy. Many of the medical staff had been sent to the front. The sick were not always attended to in time. Many perished from lack of timely treatment.

The nurse on duty took Ama from Lena's arms and told her to leave and come back the next morning. Family members were not allowed to stay with the sick. The place was overcrowded.

After a sleepless night, early in the morning, Lena trudged down to the hospital's gates. A large group was already waiting to hear the conditions of their loved ones. Entering the building was forbidden. They were waiting for the hospital's official whose duty it was to announce the names of those that did not survive the night and notify their families.

"Ama Cherfas," the announcer called, meeting Lena's anxious eyes. "She died during the night," he announced in a dry, business-like manner.

Lena, horrified, sprinted up the steps, pushed the guard aside, and started running through the hospital's corridors. There were gurneys with sick people lined up against the walls, waiting for a healing hand or death, whichever came first. Lena peered into the many faces. At the end of the hall, tied with straps to a narrow bench, she found her daughter unconscious. The straps were keeping her from falling off.

The quick morning count by the staff, checking to see who survived the night, had been carried out without a close examination. Ama, strapped to the bench, lay listless and therefore had been counted among the dead.

Lena wrapped her feverish daughter in her coat and, with no requests or explanations, marched with her outside the hospital, a place that seemed to offer very little help to the sick.

Ama had contracted malaria. They remained in the guest house for two weeks while she recovered slowly and gained her strength back.

It was difficult to maintain cleanliness and hygiene in their circumstances. The stay in the hospital, while not contributing to Ama's healing, had left her with lice. Lena decided to take drastic measures to safeguard their health and hygiene. Ama's soft light hair came off first. Lena shaved her own wavy blond hair too. A colorful kerchief became Lena's staple head covering. Ama sported a white knit cap they had brought from home.

29

If necessary, she was willing to beg

A stern face eyed the approaching young woman, who led a small child by the hand and carried a leather suitcase in her other hand. She was very thin and looked tired. The child, a little girl, wore a knit cap that had once been white. The one distinguishing feature in her small, thin face were her large green eyes that stared at the strange woman with a resigned apathy. They spoke of experiences beyond her tender age.

Lena's father had given her the addresses of relatives scattered across Russia. He knew they might come in handy. Sonia, the woman facing Lena, was a second cousin to Moshe. Their contact through the years had been sparse, but Moshe counted on his knowledge that Jews, in times of need, extended each other a helping hand.

The roads were scattered with displaced people. Some were hoping to find temporary refuge from the ravaging war by reaching relatives, distant family. They hoped to be welcomed, accepted, and given a spare corner to lay their belongings in and call a home, at least until, they hoped, safety returned, and they could head back to where they had come from.

Lena and Ama were among those people. Lena approached the stern-looking woman, a hesitant smile gracing her face. She placed her suitcase on the ground and picked her daughter up.

"I am Moshe Goldberg's daughter," started Lena. They were sitting in Sonia's kitchen, sipping a welcome cup of hot tea. "My daughter and I have come a long way, seeking to connect with family. We are alone. My husband was killed on the Latvian front. They placed him with a tank battalion. He was killed by the second week. He and the other 100,000 Latvian troops were sent to the front with no training. He was not a soldier; he was a scholar. My younger brother, Ilka, joined the Russian army. I hope that he has a better chance to survive."

Sonia felt great sympathy for the young woman, but her brow furrowed with worry. "All our men are at the front, fighting," she started. "I, my sister Anya, and our six children are barely managing to survive. Food is scarce, and our home can hardly fit us all."

"As soon as I find employment, I'll get my own place," pleaded Lena. She was a proud woman, but pride had no place in this exchange. If necessary, she was willing to beg. Frost glistened on the roof tops. The Siberian winter was approaching. Sleeping in drafty barns with three-year-old Ama was not a viable option anymore.

The temporary space Lena was offered was a corner of a long hallway in the modest home. A thin mattress was placed on the floor at night with a couple of equally thin blankets, meant to keep them relatively warm. When the cold was unbearable, Lena and Ama huddled near the coal stove in the kitchen.

The lack of substantial food and the harsh conditions during their journey finally caught up with Lena. One morning she could not get up. She had become gravely ill. Little Ama stayed on the floor, next to her feverish mother. She was determined not to let her mother die. Too many people in her young life had disappeared. She believed that by watching over her mother during her waking hours, she would prevent her mother from leaving her, too.

The other inhabitants of the house distanced themselves. Illnesses were common, especially among the population that traveled from far, unknown locations. The cousins were afraid of Lena's condition. They were concerned it might be an infectious disease. Five days later, Lena's fever broke. Her youth and determination had prevailed. She regained her health.

30

I was afraid to approach you

Bathing was a weekly ritual. The Jews were strict in adhering to that custom. It took place in the local bathhouse where, for a small fee, the visitor could use buckets of hot water to cleanse herself.

This ritual was not one of Ama's favorite pastimes. The water was too hot and the steaming bodies surrounding her were frightening to a small child.

It was Lena's first time out of the house since her recovery. She had short, cropped hair growing out of her shaven head. Her once round, beautiful face was now gaunt. She looked emaciated.

Lena noticed a woman eying her with curiosity. The woman looked familiar, but Lena could not place her. It was obvious that this person was keeping her distance. Lena still looked ill. She continued to pour hot water over Ama despite her loud protests, when she heard her name called. The strange woman was cautiously coming closer. "Lena?" she uttered. "Is that you? Lena Goldberg?"

Mira had been a friend from childhood. They had both grown up in Rēzekne. The war didn't seem to have harmed Mira. She looked well fed, and, as they were dressing, Lena took note of her fine clothes.

"I was afraid to approach you," said Mira. "What happened to you? Let's go sit on the bench outside. Tell me everything."

Mira's war experiences differed greatly from Lena's. "My brother immigrated to Ufa years ago," she started telling Lena. "When we heard that the Germans were progressing towards our borders, both my parents and I fled the country and joined my brother and his family. My parents, in their fifties now, are still alive and doing well. A short time after I arrived, I landed a great job, serving food at a Russian officers' dining club. I am a food server, so we never lack for food, and I get decent wages." That was obvious from her appearance. Mira was fashionably dressed and had a smooth, flawless complexion. "I share a home with my parents. Having my brother and his family in our lives has sustained us through these difficult years."

Lena's story had a different path. Dressed in a threadbare black coat, she smoothed her hand over the kerchief that she wore to hide her short hair. She finished sharing her war experiences with her friend. Mira remained silent. She reached out to the little girl and pulled her in for a hug. Lena stood up, poised to depart.

"Listen to me," said Mira. Tomorrow, after eight in the evening, when they close the dining hall, come by the club. Enter through the back door. I will save some leftover food for you."

"*Spasiba*" *(Thank you)*, whispered Lena. "I will meet you tomorrow."

31

Words "work" and "food" were music to Lena's ears

I t was late. The square, industrial-looking building, looming in the dark, seemed quiet. The patrons, Russian officers
who had the privilege of dining in this establishment, were leaving, singing loudly and holding onto each other in a drunken
stupor. Left behind were those who cared for its maintenance
and cleaning.

Mira stayed behind on this special night. She was determined to help Lena in any way she could. In her hand, she
held a cardboard box with leftovers she had saved. The food
came from the officers' discarded meals. Some of them suffered
from poor digestion and had no appetite for the plentiful food
on their plates.

They met outside and sat on a nearby bench. Lena's head
was again covered with a scarf, cropped hair hidden.

"Listen," said Mira, "I want you to come tomorrow, early
in the morning, and meet the woman who's in charge of the
workers. She can be a bitch and self-serving, but if you stay on
her good side, she'll treat you well. We are short of workers right
now, and she might give you some work. You will be close to
the kitchen and that means close to food."

The words "work" and "food" were music to Lena's ears. It meant she could leave her relative's meager accommodations and move with Ama to a place she could finally call home.

The work assigned to her was at night when the building was empty of people. She was to scrub the wooden floors. The work had to be done on hands and knees. It was hard work, but the extra food it provided for her and Ama—always leftovers from the lavish meals served to the officers—made it worthwhile.

The workers used to fry the leftovers at high temperatures before consuming any. The sounds of coughing and hacking coming from the dining hall were worrisome. Tuberculosis was common among the Russian troops.

Lena settled into the night job of scrubbing stubborn stains from rough wooden floors, work that would burden her with back pain for the rest of her life.

Ama stayed in their temporary accommodations while Lena was at work, sleeping on the floor on her mother's mattress in a corner of the home's hallway. Her aunts were busy with the endless chores of running a home and providing for their children. Her cousins were older and away at school. The days were long and boring, and the nights were lonely.

Lena's hard work was soon noticed, and she was promoted to a food server. Her work hours had changed. She could stay with Ama at night. The change in her work situation was significant, since food servers were treated better and paid more. She started searching for a place for her and Ama.

32

She certainly is a Goldberg, she mused

The wooden structure they were walking towards was perched on a small side street of Ufa's poorer section. It was part of a complex, hastily built to accommodate the relentless flood of refugees arriving in town, escaping their war-ravaged cities and villages. The northern regions were still considered safe.

A thin plywood partition divided the interior of each small shack, allowing two families to occupy one dwelling. The local authorities had strict control over who was allowed to live there because the cost was subsidized by the government. Many homeless families were in line, hoping to be awarded shelter. Lena was a war widow; as such she was among the fortunate. She and her daughter were assigned a small room. A plywood partition separated them from their neighbors.

Lena and Ama had stayed in their cousins' home for over six months. It was thanks to their generosity that Lena was able to recuperate after her long travels and become strong enough to embark on a new life. The few belongings they had still fit into one leather suitcase and one backpack.

She thanked their hosts for opening their home to her and Ama at a time of need. "I will forever remain grateful to you for your generosity," she said to Sonia. "I know that having two more mouths to feed added hardship. I will let my father know, when I see him, that he can be proud of the family he belongs to."

Sonia had grown fond of the young woman and the child. Lena was not a burden on their household. She was a hard worker and quick to learn. She took over the care of the few livestock they managed to sustain in the small plot behind the house. She milked the skinny cow every morning and fed the flock of chickens, while gathering their fresh eggs. Ama followed behind her, trying to grab hold of the colorful birds. Her main mission in life was not to let her mother out of her sight. She knew her survival was connected to her mother's presence, and what little control she had in her life she was determined to hold onto.

Sonia knew she'd miss Lena's pretty, young face around their dinner table, and the food Lena managed to contribute to the family's dinners. She picked up Ama and kissed her tenderly on the cheek. "Lenushka," she said, "your presence brightened our dull existence. I feel fortunate that you found us. Promise not to be a stranger. I wish you and little Ama a wonderful life in your new home." The two women hugged and promised each other to stay in touch. Sonya stood by the road and looked at their receding figures. "She certainly is a Goldberg," she mused, remembering Moshe, her cousin, and his ferociously determined nature.

33

Ama's eyes grew large and bright

Lena was employed at the officers' dining club. She was a food server now and worked during the day. Ama was about to turn four. She was bright and inquisitive. Lena had to find a safe place for her daughter during the long hours when she was at work.

"Would you like to go to a school where you'll meet other children?" asked Lena. Ama's eyes grew large and bright. The thought of joining other children in song, dance, and play excited her.

The small wooden cottage was a daycare center for children whose parents were employed by the government. Lena, a war widow and employed at the officers' cabinet, was entitled to those benefits. Stalin was not too concerned about sending untrained young men to fight the war and get killed, but he made sure that the population back home would see him as their beloved, caring leader.

This was Ama's first experience with a large group of children. She was cautious and discerning, checking out each person and situation before joining the activity.

Lena entered the cottage. The room was filled with children of preschool age. Ama was twirling around to the sound of lively music. Colorful streamers, attached to a wreath on her head, floated around her in a circle. She thrived in the company of other children, soaking up the sense of comradery and friendship. Though the trials of her early years had left her somber and quiet, her new surroundings created a safe place where she slowly began to relax.

Lena was on a short break. In her hand she carried a jar filled with porridge, a leftover treasure from the officers' breakfast. She was trying to convince Ama to consume the food she had brought. In the past she would have left the food with the women who cared for the children, asking the caretakers to feed it to Ama at mealtimes. The preschool only offered a coco drink and a slice of bread with jam. She soon realized that the food was indeed consumed, but not by Ama. She decided to come on her short break and feed her daughter herself. The hurried force-feeding didn't go well. Ama developed diarrhea. The outhouse was at the end of the property, and she often didn't make it in time.

Winter arrived and, with it, freezing weather. The small wood stove in the corner of the daycare was not adequate to keep the place warm. The cold wind blowing outside forced its way through the cracks around the windows and doors. The children huddled near the stove. There was no motivation to sing and dance. The one cup of hot coco was the highlight of the day. Ama, at the age of four, still sometimes wet her pants, especially in the chilly weather. She would end up staying hours in wet, cold clothes.

A call for Lena came from the daycare center. She was asked to come immediately. She found Ama lying listless on a blanket. Her face was swollen. She was burning up with fever. The wet clothes and the chill in the room had resulted in a severe kidney infection.

Lena was determined not to leave Ama's care to an institutional center. It was all she could afford, but the health of her daughter was at stake, and this place was not providing optimal caregiving. It was a place to park a child so the parent could go serve Mother Russia for meager pay.

34

They are a match made in heaven

Gedalya and his wife, Ela, were Lena's neighbors. A thin wooden ply separated their two quarters. It was a poor barrier. Conversation and the clank of dishes could be heard on both sides.

They were in their forties—he, previously a wealthy merchant, and she, a music teacher. They had fled Moscow when it became a war zone. Ela was a gifted pianist who, before the war, was part of Moscow's philharmonic orchestra. Gedalya ran a large feed store, supplying the needs of local farmers. He was among the first to be drafted. At 40 he was not normally considered of drafting age, but in October 1941, when the German forces were gaining and advancing towards Moscow, he was called to join the fighting forces. A hand grenade exploded near the ditch he was burrowed in. A piece of shrapnel embedded in his spine left him paralyzed from the neck down. Upon his release from the hospital, the couple chose to escape the embattled city and find themselves a new home.

Ela was now employed as a caretaker for a wealthy Russian household. She was gone for long hours during the day. Gedalya depended on others for his needs. To ensure his care during the day Ela hired an elderly woman to check on him several times a day. The rest of the time he was left to his thoughts and memories.

Ama's bout with kidney infection at the day-care center made Lena reconsider the benefits of leaving her daughter in the care of those who, for meager pay, served as glorified babysitters without much attention or care for the children. Lena decided to leave Ama at home, and Gedalya's presence was a Godsend. His watchful eye, sitting in his wheelchair in the middle of the small courtyard, gave her some assurance for her daughter's safety. In the middle of the courtyard stood a deep well that caused Lena concern, although it was encased in a low stone wall for protection.

Gedalya sat in his wheelchair in the middle of the small courtyard surrounded by wooden sheds. Ama stepped toward him and climbed on his lap. She held a children's book with colorful pictures and slowly turned the pages. "Can you read me the stories?" she asked. The sudden presence of the little girl in Gedalya's life was like a ray of sunshine in his lonely existence.

Listening to Gedalya's voice as he read, Ama leaned her head on his shoulder. She loved listening to stories, and he, as it turned out, loved reading them to her.

"They are a match made in heaven," thought Lena, watching them through the small window of her room. "He is a good man. I think she will be safe under his watch when I am at work." Only the looming, deep well, in the middle of the court, filled her with dread.

Gedalya and Ama developed a beautiful friendship. Through her eyes he saw himself as a whole man. His disabilities didn't cause her to see him as less than the wonderful caring person he was. "Why are you sitting in this chair all day?" she asked. "Because I can't move my legs," answered Gedalya.

"Hmm..." mused Ama. "Did you fall and get hurt? Does it still hurt? Are you sad because you cannot run and jump?" She continued her inquiries, stroking his knee with concern.

"Some bad people hurt me, but I am not in pain, and because you are here keeping me company, I am not sad anymore."

Ama considered his answer and felt a deep sense of satisfaction. She asked frank questions and he was candid with his answers. With his teeth he managed to unbutton her pants when she needed to go to the bathroom, and she brought him odds and ends when he requested. They shared a love for visual images. Ama loved drawing, and, to her delight, she discovered that she shared that love with Gedalya. She brought him pages of white paper, and, with a pencil she placed between his teeth, he drew her pictures of animals, trees, and flowers.

35

I judged that little Jew right, she thought

Gospojha Olga oversaw the running of the cabinet, the officers' dining hall. In her mid-fifties, she was a war widow. Her husband had been among the first casualties of the war. The authorities awarded her a desirable position in appreciation for her loss and her husband's contribution to the country's war efforts.

She was a stout woman with a ruddy complexion. Her size was evidence of a comfortable life with plenty of food. Being childless had left her lonely and, unfortunately, without much empathy for the people that were under her command. She carefully chose the ones she treated favorably. They had to earn it.

Lena was gaining weight. Her blonde hair got longer and her blue eyes brighter. Her good looks returned. This did not escape her boss's eye. Olga knew that the Russian officers liked to have pretty women serve them. She eyed Lena carefully and tried to assess her measure of obedience and loyalty.

Lena, as a food server, was now working in the main dining hall. It was time for Olga to get her payoff. The first test came shortly after Lena's promotion. She was called into Olga's office.

It was a grand room, lavish, with a comfortable sofa clad in blue velvet and a thick hand-knotted rug on the gleaming wooden floor planks. The corner sported a small kitchen, its shelves bursting with a bounty of food items Lena hadn't seen since she left home: cans of milk, small bags of sugar, coffee, and coco. Olga was seated at a large wooden desk, her hefty chin leaning on her hands.

"You are a good worker," she said to Lena. "You can advance quickly in our organization. There are a few jobs I will need you to do outside of this place, in your own time. Those special jobs need to remain between you and me. No one else is supposed to know anything about what I am asking you to do. Is that clear?"

Lena was cautious. She knew that whatever it was her boss was going to expect of her could not be legal. Bribing and stealing were a way of life in Russian culture. People knew how to skirt the authorities. Getting caught condemned you to a lifetime term in a Siberian prison, never to be heard of or seen again. She quickly weighed her options.

Olga was leaning comfortably back in her chair, like a queen on a throne. She was gazing at Lena with steely, emotionless eyes; Lena knew that her survival was in this person's hands. Refusing would cause her to lose her job. Her and her daughter's lives had improved immensely after she got her current position. They had relaxed into an existence that provided them adequate food and shelter.

"What is it that I can be of help with?" she asked. "I will do any job you assign to me inside the building or elsewhere."

A satisfied grin spread across Olga's ample face. "I judged that little Jew right," she thought. "She will be subservient to my command."

Lena was instructed to carry out Olga's requests at night, in the dark, after her working hours. She was ordered to carry a large backpack to Olga's residence. The bag contained sugar, butter, eggs, chocolate and, at times, other food items, all stolen from the food rations allocated by the government for the officers' meals.

At night Lena walked the long miles silently, moving like a shadow. The temperature plummeting below freezing. The snow was ankle deep, the pack on her back heavy. Military vehicles randomly combed the streets. Black market dealings were rampant. When faced with hunger and deprivation, people found ways to outsmart the law.

A vehicle stopped behind Lena's plodding figure. A young man in uniform called after her, "You, stop." Lena's shoulders drooped. She felt the old familiar sensation at the pit of her stomach. Fear gripped her body. She knew that, if she were caught and charged with smuggling, she'd never see her daughter again. "What's in that large pack on your back, *devushka" (young lady)*? asked the soldier.

"I am moving to a new place," answered Lena, scrambling quickly to come up with a reasonable story for carrying a huge pack in the dark. "My little daughter is waiting for me. I am slowly carrying our belongings from where we used to live. I can only do it at night. I work at the officers' cabinet and am employed during the day." She finished her long explanation and batted her lashes, coyly staring at the young man.

"Officers' cabinet, huh?" repeated the soldier. "They get all the good food while we lowlifes, who do all the grunge work, get the leftover slop. "If I meet you outside the building, could you sneak me some food? I am getting tired of the porridge and potatoes we are being served daily at our camp."

Lena answered hesitantly, "Come tomorrow to the back entrance. I will meet you there. I'll even sneak you a chocolate bar," she added with a dazzling smile.

"Great," answered the guy. "Go on your way and be more careful. Most of the guys driving around are not as gullible as me," he added with a wink.

The trek to Olga's cottage was two miles long, up a country road. She lived in a small cottage with a cozy fireplace and two comfortable bedrooms. It was furnished with the best Russia had to offer in times of peace. She had obviously learned how to manipulate these times of crisis in her favor.

36

Mama said never to open the door to anyone

It was getting dark. Ama and Gedalya had spent some splendid hours together discussing important issues like what was her favorite food and what did he like to do before he was injured. Ela, back from her day job, wheeled Gedalya to their side of the dwelling to proceed with their evening routine. Ama collected her books, entered their room, and locked the door. She knew to wait for her mother when she was home alone. "Always keep the door locked and never open it to anyone when I am away," Lena had stressed to her four-year-old daughter. She was, at times, held up at the dining hall for extra needed chores.

Ama munched on dry biscuits and lay on the wood floor with paper and colored pencils. She immersed herself in a make-believe world, a world with sunshine, blue sky, flowers, and butterflies. Invariably, she laid her head down on her worn blanket and fell asleep.

There was a loud knock on the door. Ama, startled from her sleep, remained quiet. The persistent knocking alarmed her. She crouched by the door and listened.

"Amichka," came a familiar voice from the other side of the door. "It's me, Ilka. Open the door sweetheart."

Ama's eyes grew wide. She recognized this man's voice. She loved him and was excited to hear his voice. She stared thoughtfully at the door and answered, "I cannot open the door. Mama said never to open the door to anyone."

Some pleading and cajoling followed. "I am your uncle. It is fine for you to open the door to me. Mama will be happy to see me."

"Mama said never to open the door to anyone," repeated Ama firmly with her ear pressed to the door.

Upon returning home, Lena found a sleeping soldier on the doorstep to her home and a tired little girl sleeping on the floor on the other side of the door.

Their reunion was joyous. Ilka was on leave again. This was the second time he had been injured on the battlefield, both times in the same leg. His limping was very pronounced. He needed the aid of a cane to walk.

Out of his suitcase he pulled a small rubber duck and handed it to Ama, who took it with a shy smile. Lena's eyes grew wide when he handed her a pair of shiny brown leather boots lined with fur. This was a luxury beyond her dreams. He knew her foot size, and the boots fit her feet perfectly. Her joy was mixed with worry. She stared at his large case filled with assorted goods and gave him a reproachful look. Ilka, while on leave from his army service to recuperate from his injuries, was engaged in shady activities.

She knew that he was probably trading for these items illegally. Being caught with such merchandise purchased on the black market was a punishable offense. Ilka was planning to stash his goods at Lena's, most likely under her bed. This would make her an accomplice and place her in danger too.

Ilka gave his sister a squeeze and tried to ease her concerns. "I have been dealing in the black market for months," he said. "They are too dumb to catch up to me. Too dumb and too drunk." The challenging times, as well as the inherent Russian culture, drove people to consume large amounts of vodka, which softened the misery of their lives.

His stories of his travels and the progress of the war were exciting news. It was early 1945. An intensive aerial bombardment by the Allied forces preceded a land invasion of Germany. The end of this nightmare became a possibility.

Neither of them had heard any news of their loved ones. Ilka somberly repeated rumors he had heard from displaced refugees arriving from the Baltics. The Germans' methods of asserting their occupation and authority on regions they conquered were chilling. Fear gripped Lena's heart, thinking of her father's possible fate.

Ilka's face was drawn and tired. "He has aged so much," thought Lena, studying her 23-year-old brother. "This bloody war has robbed us both of our youth," she thought bitterly. Lena was a pragmatic thinker, mostly directing attention to the chores in front of her. Occupying her thoughts with "what ifs" was not in her nature. This was different. So much was at stake. Imagining the worst possibilities gripped her heart.

The room was heated with a small masonry stove, its round top doubling as a cooking surface. The three huddled around it. Ama, seated on Ilka's knees, was stuck to him like a barnacle. She stroked the stubble on his cheeks and stared into his blue eyes. She vaguely remembered being held and rocked by him eons ago. His firm hold on her little body felt so familiar. It gave her a feeling of safety. She missed being held in that manner.

In the couple of pans Lena owned, with a few mixing utensils, she prepared a hearty meal, happy to have food she had brought from work, leftovers from the officers' meals. Wrapped in woolen shawls, they basked in each other's company while enjoying the hot broth and buckwheat porridge, a staple on Lena's table.

A couple of blankets spread in a corner of Lena's room served as a bed for Ilka. His travels had caught up with him. He spent much of the time catching up on his rest. Traveling through Russian towns while on leave had kept him very busy. During times of human disaster, those with cunning resourcefulness managed to benefit from the circumstances. Ilka was not above taking advantage of a situation. The black market was thriving.

The loss of the occupied territories created severe shortages. People were starving. Some were living on a single bowl of cabbage soup a day. Food shortages prompted black markets to sprout and theft to rule, starting with petty pillaging and progressing to large-scale embezzlement.

The Kolkhoz was an idea established by the Russian government—the creation of Soviet collective farms. All grown produce became the property of the government. Mother Russia needed all the supplies she could gather. The farmers were to contribute their crops to support the fighting troops. They were allowed to keep a small amount of what they grew to feed their families and bring to market for sale. The incentive for production diminished considerably. Lena was astonished at the puny fruits and vegetables displayed on the market stalls. To her, the potatoes looked no bigger than plums. There was little motivation to work hard and produce healthy crops.

Limiting what the farmers could keep of what they grew for feeding their families and sell for profit contributed to the spreading of the black market, where people could buy rationed items on the sly, but at higher prices. Many were engaged in illegal means to make ends meet. The markets swarmed with shady exchanges.

Ilka, bright and resourceful, learned quickly how to maneuver through the system, moving carefully and skirting the law. The suitcase he'd brought with him to Lena's apartment was full of illegally acquired merchandise. He tucked the case deep under Lena's cot.

37

Alcohol was a great motivator in the Russian army

Next day, early in the morning, there was an insistent knocking on Lena's door. It was Sunday. The three of them were sitting around a small wooden table in the corner of the makeshift kitchen, enjoying each other's company and feasting on the tasty corn cakes Lena had prepared. The small amount of butter and sugar she sneaked from the officers' lounge kitchen added to their delight.

At the sound of the knocking Lena looked at Ilka, alarmed. He placed a finger to his lips signaling for her and Ama to remain quiet. "Who is it?" he demanded.

"Comrade Goldberg," came a voice from the door, "it's Officer Vasiliev. Open the door. I am here on official business."

The short, uniformed officer walked into the room, trying to look as important as possible. He placed himself comfortably on Lena's bed, the only additional sitting space in the room. The cot caved under his ample weight. The prevailing shortage of food didn't seem to have affected him. His face glistened with sweat. Climbing the hill leading to the small dwelling was an effort. He tucked his short legs deep under the bed. Lena's breath was caught in her throat. His boots were inches from the suitcase.

"*Tovarich* Goldberg" *(Comrade),* the officer opened in a nasal voice, "you have caught the attention of the authorities. There are reports that you are engaged in illegal activities. I am here to ask you questions and search the premises."

Lena's eyes dropped to the floor. If Ilka's merchandise was found under her bed, she would be considered an accomplice and dealt with accordingly.

Ilka cocked his head to one side and, with a broad smile, approached the seated man and placed a friendly hand on his shoulder. In his other hand he held a bottle full of vodka.

Alcohol was a great motivator in the Russian army. It was offered to soldiers to relieve nervous tension and enhance their mood. Officer Vassiliev's eyes shone with delight. The offering was much appreciated, and he had no intention of refusing it on account of being on official business. The conversation flowed in a friendly manner. Ilka was well versed on how to stroke the egos of those he needed on his side. He kept refilling the officer's cup to the brim while praising him and the whole Russian army for their incredible war efforts.

"Tovarich Goldberg," droned on Vassiliev. His speech was quite slurred by now, his thinking impaired. "This time I'll just give you a warning. They are on to you. You are a nice young man. Take my warning to heart and stop your illegal activities."

He took another gulp of vodka from his cup. His eyes fell on Lena's feet. "Ohhh," he exclaimed, "those are some fine boots. They look just about my wife's size." Ilka rushed to Lena and pulled the boots off her feet.

"Here you are, Tovarich, a gift for your wife. Take them. They'll make her very happy." The officer touched his cap in appreciation, bowed respectfully to Lena and stumbled towards the door, clutching Lena's boots to his chest.

The room fell into darkness. They remained quiet. No one spoke for a while. Lena cast a long reproachful glance at her brother and a mournful look at her bare feet.

38

She raised herself on tiptoes and kissed him

Lena placed a steaming plate of food on the table in front of an officer who was sitting alone by a window. He looked into her eyes and thanked her. He had a kind face with sad eyes.

She had noticed him before. He always sat by himself. He didn't join in the often raucous exchanges among the other officers.

In the coming weeks she saw him often, always sitting alone at the same table, eating his meals alone, preferring his solitude over the comradery most officers were after. One day, when she served him his meal, he stopped her, touched her hand gently and asked, "Would you tell me your name and where you come from?"

"I'm sorry," she answered. "I can't stay and talk to you." He felt her hesitation and reluctance to have any association with him.

Lena could sense his loneliness, but she couldn't stop to talk. She was expected in the kitchen. Engaging in a friendly conversation with one of the officers was frowned upon. She excused herself and retreated to the kitchen.

Lieutenant Ivanov was tall and slightly built. He had a soft voice and kind eyes. The mysterious and beautiful young woman had captured Ivanov's heart. He looked after her retreating figure and was suddenly overcome by great sadness. He knew that they were worlds apart and that his chances to have her respond to him were slim to none. He looked forward to their short meetings at mealtimes and their fleeting exchanges.

Several weeks had passed. Ivanov decided to venture out. "I would very much like to spend some time with you away from this place. Would you be willing to join me on a walk?" He looked anxiously into Lena's eyes.

She was expecting this and had given it considerable thought before it happened. "I don't see how that would cause any problem if we were away from these premises," she answered. "My working hours are long, and I hurry home to my little daughter, who is alone, so the walk needs to be a short one," she added.

"I can pick you up next Sunday when the cabinet is closed," answered Ivanov. "Bring your little daughter. I'd love to meet her." Lena agreed. She was lonely. His attention made her feel alive and desired.

Lieutenant Ivanov was from Petersburg and, like Micha, Lena's deceased husband, he was a scholar, not a soldier. Before the war he taught literature to high-school children. He loved his work and was saddened when his country called him to serve. His intelligence and education awarded him a rapid climb in the ranks.

After a few months, their acquaintance grew into a tender friendship. Spring brought a welcome change. The river was full of fish. A thick carpet of wildflowers covered its shores. An orchestra of bird song could be heard from the branches of the white-trunked birch trees. There was a delicious fragrance in the air. It was easy to believe that a better future was around the corner.

Lena and Ivanov found comfort and joy in each other's company. She enjoyed his intelligence, reminding her so much of Micha. He admired her courage and fierce spirit, qualities that had sustained her and enabled her miraculous survival. He realized that he had fallen in love with this feisty little woman

On one of their walks Ivanov turned to Lena and gazed longingly into her eyes. He was acutely aware of their differences, and yet he hesitantly reached out and took her hand in his. "Lena, I want to take care of you and your little daughter," he said in a quiet voice. "I want to give you a good life. I don't want you to work in that wretched place, for meager pay. I love you. I want you to be my wife." He promised her and her child security and a good life.

Lena had developed feelings for this kind man, maybe even love. However, only one thought occupied her mind. To survive the war and return to her people. She searched Ivanov's face and sighed. "You are a wonderful person with a beautiful kind heart. Our lives have different paths. I don't intend to stay in this country with these people. I intend to join my own people in our country. You deserve someone who belongs here. I do not." She raised herself on her tiptoes and kissed him gently on his cheek, squeezed his hand, turned around, and walked away.

39

The journey back home

It was Tuesday morning. A glorious spring day welcomed Ama when she opened her eyes and looked around the room. She didn't see her mother. It was Lena's day off. She had put in many hours the day before, serving a large party of officers and other dignitaries who were celebrating with vodka and good food. Germany's imminent defeat was in the air. Their economy and productivity were plummeting. Their supply lines were weakened due to attacks by the Allied forces and ambushes carried out by partisan groups. Hitler had retreated to his hiding place and left weak leadership in his wake. The German army was spread thin on two fronts. The Russian winter had been brutal. Temperatures plunged to 40 degrees below zero, freezing soldiers, tanks, and equipment. Coats, hats, boots, and gloves needed for the soldiers were not arriving due to the destroyed supply lines.

Ama heard voices from outside their room. She peeked through the small window. Her mother; Gedalya, his wife, Ela; and other neighbors were cheering, laughing, and speaking in loud excited voices. Ama exited their front door. Lena rushed over, picked up her daughter and carried her into the center of the group. Arms reached out to stroke her hair and kiss her on her cheek. Spirits were high. Some were wiping tears of joy.

The date was May 8, 1945. The group was celebrating the end of the bloodiest war in history. A war that lasted six years and a day. A war that killed more than 60 million people, most of them civilians, many through the most systematic genocide in modern history. Cities and towns were destroyed by aerial bombing and heavy artillery. Every household in Europe had suffered losses.

The expression that grew out of that period, "Never Again," symbolized a universal desire to never let such a senseless and destructive occurrence grip civilization again.

The time had come for Lena to plan the third stage of their journey, the journey back home. Ilka advised her to let events in Europe settle first and let spirits calm down. The next few months were spent in preparations and anticipation for the trip back home. She felt apprehensive about what awaited her back in her birth country.

The parting from Gedalya, Ela, and Mira was emotional. Mira was planning to stay in Ufa, a place that had been kind to her, supplying her with a good life and a man she'd married and built a home with. Lena held her in a long embrace, whispering thanks in her ear. Mira had saved her life when she and Ama arrived in Ufa, tired, sick, and very poor. Thanks to her prompting and recommendation, Lena got employment that supplied her and her daughter with food and shelter.

Gedalya and Ela were headed back to Moscow, their home place. A flicker of hope was rekindled in people's hearts, a hope to find survivors, friends, and family they had left behind. Ama climbed on her friend's paralyzed knees. She held his head in an embrace and whispered: "*Ya tee lublu* "(*I love you*). She told him that she was going to miss him and that she would write him letters with pictures. Gedalya kissed her cheek. "You are going to grow up to be a great storyteller, Amichka. Keep reading and practice your drawing. I know you'll be an artist too."

Late in December 1945, clad in their warmest clothes, Lena and Ama walked towards the train station. They were heading back to Riga, venturing on a 2,300-kilometer ride alone, leaving behind a life they had built and learned to trust. The time they spent in Ufa gained them friends that had sustained them for the last two years and left them with sweet human experiences that helped Lena heal and regain her strength.

They were heading back to their homeland, not knowing what and who they would find. Lena hoped to reunite with family and rebuild her life that had lain shattered for the last five years. For Ama this would be a new life experience, different from the one she was born into.

40

He is gone, he whispered. They killed him.

They arrived in Riga by train. Lena got off hesitantly, holding Ama's hand. Her eyes swept as much of the train's platform as she could see. It had been five years since their escape. She was apprehensive about what she would find upon her return.

Ilka had promised to greet them at the station and there he was, as handsome as ever, running towards them with open arms, his limp still pronounced. He wore a brown leather jacket and brown knee-high boots. His hair was sprinkled with white now. Deep grooves lined the corners of his eyes that, by the young age of 25, had seen too much destruction and pain. Lena ran towards his approaching form, dragging Ama by her arm.

His embrace was grounding, promising safety and security. He was her kid brother, but he was all grown up now and appeared strong. His presence infused her with reassurance and hope. Ilka bent down and scooped Ama into his arms. He kissed her on both cheeks and nuzzled her face. She melted into his embrace, inhaling his familiar scent.

Lena felt lightheaded. The sight of the destruction in the streets was heart wrenching. Riga was known for its beautiful architecture, lush parks, and blossoming gardens. Majestic buildings were now replaced by mounds of debris and dust. She remembered strolling through these avenues with her mother on their shopping trips. What she saw had no resemblance to the Riga she remembered and loved.

She looked at Ilka urgently with inquiring eyes. He knew what she wanted to know without asking. "He is gone, Lenichka," he whispered. "They killed him." They sat on a park bench and held hands. He told her that their father had been killed in the first weeks of the German occupation and held her tight, trying to calm her heartbroken sobs.

41

The victims lined up against the wall

The Peitav Synagogue stood in the center of Riga. The impressive structure was built in 1903 in the Art Nouveau style. Its location near other municipal buildings had saved it from destruction. All the other synagogues in town had been systematically burned by the Nazis and their Latvian collaborators during the first days of the occupation.

The synagogue is one of the most important institutions in Judaism; it is viewed as the heart of the community, and that is where many Jewish families who fled their homes after the Nazi invasion sought refuge. The belief that a place of worship will be respected by all was very quickly dispelled. The Jews were burned inside the buildings.

There were 210 synagogues in Latvia before World War II, with styles ranging from ornate Neo-Renaissance and Neo-Romanesque to humble wooden structures. After the war only two remained standing.

In the fall of 1945, Jews returning to Riga, their homeland, quickly learned that the Peitav synagogue had been established as a center for the surviving Latvian Jews, a place to gather and find connections, to get help with accommodations and meet lost relatives, or at least to learn about their fate.

Not all the Jewish population had left Latvia. Some escaped Nazi persecution by hiding in obscure places across the land.

They were aided by Latvian citizens, human beings who hadn't lost their humanity and sense of justice.

Lena and Ilka were heading to the Peitav. They saw groups of people huddled on the front steps. Some were clad in *tallits* (prayer shawls), praying to a God that had spared them while abandoning so many others. The human spirit started to emerge again. Hope for a brighter future was in the air and, for some, the surest way to secure that outcome was still in prayers.

They saw faces, vaguely familiar. Most of those that survived were young, but the war years had not been kind. The suffering from loss, hunger, homelessness, and persecution etched deep grooves in their young faces. They had aged in an untimely manner.

The reunion was emotional for Lena. She saw people from her town, Rēzekne. They shared detailed stories of the mass murders that were carried out by the Nazis.

By July 1941, The Nazi regime had embarked on a process of elimination of the Jewish population in Latvia. These persecutions were carried out by special units made of eager Latvian citizen volunteers. The Nazi occupiers didn't need to have a large presence. Latvian collaborators quickly learned how to oppress, steal, and murder efficiently. They willingly assumed the function of the Nazi authorities in the elimination of their fellow countrymen, their Jewish friends and neighbors.

Lena learned that her father, a respected citizen of the Jewish community, had been ordered to sweep the streets of the town. One day the Nazi authorities gathered a group of the remaining Jews in Rēzekne and marched them to the central square. Moshe Goldberg was among them. A mob of Latvians gathered around the square, some apprehensive about what was taking place, and some anticipating the opportunity to loot and rob the residences of those about to be executed. The victims lined up against the wall, stripped of all power and human dignity, had been their neighbors and friends. Many were indebted to Moshe for extending them credit while shopping in his store. The soldiers ordered the men to form a line, pushing the slow-moving elders. Orders in German filled the air. The firing squad was instructed to form a line facing the victims. The distinguished figure of the town's rabbi stood erect, directing a blazing gaze at his executioners. Abe Leibovich, one of the town's elders, sank to his knees and fell unconscious.

A man stepped out of the group that was witnessing the proceedings. He carried himself with pride. It was the town's mayor. He turned to the German officer and said, "Please, mein herr (sir), these are respectful citizens of our community. Do not proceed with this insane act." He was not able to continue with his pleading. He collapsed to the ground, blood pouring from a blow to his head, inflicted by a soldier's rifle.

The dead were buried in a mass grave on the outskirts of town. There was no way of finding the final place of rest for Moshe Goldberg. He had been 57 years old.

Approximately 70,000 Latvian Jews had been eliminated. The Jewish population in Rēzekne before the beginning of the war was 6,000, Upon returning to their hometown at the end of the war, Lena and Ilka discovered that 5,000 of them had been murdered.

42

Six years of fleeing the German grip was replaced by a need to flee the Russian fist

The large flat Lena and Ama were assigned to housed three families. The one room they were given was bright and airy with windows facing the busy street. Two small cots and a sparse collection of useful furniture were adequate for their daily needs. A shared kitchen was used by all with good humor and comradery. Most of the survivors were young, tired of the war years, eager to embark on a new life. Their stay in this apartment brought them one step closer to their goal.

After their military conquest, Russia's grip on the population, including the newly conquered Baltic States, was fierce. Their regime enforced ideological and political dogmas. The Latvian language was forbidden. Those who resisted were quickly eliminated. They were imprisoned or sent to Siberia to work camps—often never to be heard from again.

Large-scale illegal immigration began. People fled to Sweden and Germany. Stalin closed the borders. No crossing was allowed into countries outside of the Soviet Union unless you were in possession of credible documents. Six years of fleeing the German grip was replaced by a need to flee the Russian fist. The quest for a new free life led to creative ways of outsmarting the authorities.

Ilka was part of a central organization, *"Bricha (Escape),"* that greeted the returning survivors and helped them plan their future. He played a major role in this group. His drawing skills helped create false documents for the travelers. His many acquaintances across the Russian states helped in finding contacts to aid the escapees find accommodation and transportation along their routes. His charismatic nature attracted men and women alike. His easy nature and quick humor were engaging. Young girls eyed him with hopes for a relationship. His mission was clear. "No Jew is left behind." He remained in Latvia until every person with the intention to escape was out of the Soviets' reach.

Their apartment became a gathering place. Many of Lena's hometown friends and acquaintances had found their way back and now were eager to meet, reminisce about the past, share war experiences, and confide in each other about the future. Lena had a clear view of hers. She was going to Israel, the homeland of her people. She longed to reunite with her two older brothers and their families. They were all she had left.

The gatherings were joyous. They shared meals of boiled potatoes and herring. The vodka poured. There was a mood of celebration and hope.

Ama was the only child in that group. Lena took her to be checked by Dr. Horowitz, who was a family friend and her doctor since she was a little girl. Dr. Horowitz had a kind face and a full head of silver hair. He picked Ama up and set her on the examining table. He looked into the little girl's eyes. She stared back at him with a brazen look. She didn't like being poked and was short of trust.

"Well," he said after examining her, "she is in fine health. You deserve a medal for getting her through this treacherous war. It is a miracle that she is in such good health."

Lena looked at him with relief and mused to herself. "I saved her life and she saved mine," she thought. "Her care and survival were the only things that mattered. They fueled me with the ability to stay alive and keep going."

"And you, Lenushka," continued the doctor, "how did you fare these last five years? You are as good looking as I remember you. You are young and strong with your mother's genes. She was a grand lady with a formidable life force. Go live a great life. Try to leave the sad past behind. He embraced Lena and stroked Ama's head.

The frequent gatherings at Lena's apartment left Ama bored. She didn't take part in the conversations and the high spirits induced mainly by the vodka. She roamed through the rooms, looking for ways to occupy herself.

Part of a girl's attire used to be a tidy little apron. That was the custom, and Ama was wearing a blue one adorned with frills. In the corner of the main gathering room, she discovered a hotplate with red gleaming spirals. These were used for cooking and, at times, to add some warmth to the rooms on chilly days. When she turned around, she discovered that the end of her apron's tie had landed on the hotplate. She stared at it in fascination, watching the cloth touch the red spirals without any consequence. She didn't try to remove it. Suddenly the fabric burst into flames. Ama, startled, tore the apron off her body, bundled the smoldering garment into a ball and stuffed it behind an open door among other stored items. Smoke started to engulf the apartment. People ran through the rooms trying to locate its source.

"*Pazharnik*" means "fireman" in Russian. That was the nickname Ama was given. For years to come, when she was a mother herself, Lena's friends, who shared and remembered that experience, would kiddingly address her by that nickname.

43

She looked at the gathered guests and declared...

A small hut in the middle of a garden served as a daycare center for children of young working families as well as those who had recently returned to Riga and lacked a permanent place of residence. It was under the strict scrutiny of the Russian authorities. The curriculum at the daycare center was heavily influenced by communist propaganda.

The establishment of a brutal communist regime resulted in the extinction of civil society and civil liberties. The demand for complete transformation of language, religious affiliation, and political alliance was unrelenting. Communist rule during Stalin's reign systematically repressed Latvian culture and way of life.

Lena and Ama walked into the daycare. Children were sitting in a circle holding hands and singing. The walls were decorated with colorful posters depicting Russian propaganda. It all looked quite cheerful. The little girls had wreaths on their heads with colorful streamers hanging down their backs. The atmosphere was gay, and Ama smiled up at her mother and nodded her head. Lena felt confident in leaving her daughter in this place.

Five-year-old Ama was, surprisingly, a happy child. She relished her new life, a life without hunger or thirst. A life without drafty barns. Her beloved uncle was a frequent visitor, and several other adults, friends of the Goldberg family, became her extended family.

She enjoyed the company of other children and joined in the singing, mostly songs about beautiful mother Russia and wonderful father Stalin, songs ordered to be taught to children from the onset of their education. However, underneath all these celebratory poems and songs she could feel the ominous presence of control. Even though she was too young to understand what that meant, she instinctively developed a dislike for it.

The first day of May, the celebration of workers, was a festive event across Russia and its occupied states. Posters depicting portraits of the "beloved" leaders, Stalin and Lenin, were carried by marchers. Songs praising mother Russia and Father Stalin were sung in the streets by the marchers.

Ama's care center planned a befitting celebration with the presence of local dignitaries. The place was decorated in colorful flags and, again, pictures of Stalin and Lenin, the "adored" leaders.

Ama was advanced for her age. Her years growing up in Ufa, speaking only the Russian language, made her the perfect candidate. She was chosen to recite a poem honoring the beloved country and its leaders under whom her people were oppressed.

She was to stand on a chair, face the crowd and, in a bright, strong voice, deliver the lovely poem. Ama got on the chair. She stood for a long while and stared at the sea of heads with a look she had perfected in the presence of Russian authorities. Under the pressure of interrogation, she would adopt the blank expression of the deaf and dumb. When she was prompted by one of her teachers, she looked at the gathered guests and declared: "*Ya zabila*" (*I forgot*) and, without any hesitation, got off the chair.

This was Ama's first encounter with passive resistance. By the age of five she had developed a deep dislike of authority, a distrust that accompanied her for the rest of her life.

44

Even small triumphs were important

Lena traveled 130 miles by train, determined to visit her mother's grave and revisit her family's home, the home she grew up in.

The sights zooming by the train's window were familiar to her. Small rolling hills graced the plains. The Rēzekne river, glistening majestically along the train's tracks, brought back childhood memories and made her think of the time she nearly drowned. That was when she had fallen in love with Ilia, the man she got engaged to, the one she so tragically lost.

Rēzekne, as a border between east and west, has served as history's battleground for over a thousand years. It has been destroyed and rebuilt by everyone from German knights in the 13th century to the warring Nazis and Russians who flattened it during World War II. The destruction of her beloved city was devastating and made Lena want to escape and return to Riga, but she had a plan, and she was determined to go through with it.

There was a strange woman standing in the middle of the Goldberg's residence. The house her father had built, the only place she knew as home, stood sad and neglected. It had been confiscated after the Russian occupation and awarded to a Russian official. He lived there with his wife and four children. There were chickens strutting in the yard. A large pig wallowed in a mud puddle. The beautiful, immaculately cared-for home she remembered was in disrepair. Peeling paint and broken shutters gave the house a disheveled appearance.

Lena met the eyes of the short, fat woman hanging wash on a line stretched between two trees, the lilac trees her father had planted. When they bloomed, the whole house was filled with their sweet scent. Lena's mother, Moshe's wife, had loved those trees. She would bring a few blossoming branches into the house and place them in water to adorn their kitchen table.

The woman's gaze was filled with suspicion. Lena didn't stay. She had a plan.

Before their hasty departure at the onset of the Nazi occupation, Lena had buried some items of value in their backyard, among them, a set of silverware, a wedding gift for her and Micha's wedding. Their initials were carved on the handles. She decided to come back at night to try to find the buried items.

Walking through the streets of her town, the destruction left by the war was apparent. Rubble and partially broken walls littered the streets. The site of her school was vacant. The shop where her father's store used to be now housed a butcher. Heads of pigs and upside-down chickens were hanging at the front of the establishment, their feet spread, pointing towards the sky in protest. A sign above the front door now read "Petrovich's Butcher Shop," replacing the one that had read "Goldberg's Fabric Store."

She stood across the street, gazing at the building, envisioning her father sweeping the sidewalk in front of his store looking up at her, smiling and waving his hand in greeting. A loud sound from the street corner brought her back to the present. A group of men were exiting a local tavern. They were drunk, and she hurried away, wiping her tears.

When night came, Lena stealthily approached her family home, hoping that all its inhabitants were in a deep sleep. With a shovel in her hand, she proceeded to the backyard, trying to remember the exact location of the buried items. Five years had passed since they fled their home. The appearance of the pristine backyard her father cultivated had changed. Weeds and brambles replaced neat beds of flowering bushes. The chickens and pigs, roaming freely in the yard, had turned the soil to mud.

Lena concentrated. She was trying to pinpoint the exact location of the buried items. When she buried them there had been no time for contemplation. She had to dig a hole in haste and drop in the heirlooms just hours before they fled and embarked on their journey.

Her eyes swept the small yard's perimeter. She saw an indentation in the ground close to the fence. "That's it," she exclaimed to herself. "That's where I buried them."

She started digging in the muddy soil. There were loud snores coming from the house and chickens' clucking from the pen. She didn't have to dig for long. The items were buried in a shallow pit, covered with soil and leaves. Unearthing the silverware was a small feat. In Lena's world, a world that had taken away people she loved and things she owned and cherished, even small triumphs were important.

45

The earth seemed so vibrant,
as if nurtured by the blood

The Jewish cemetery had been desecrated. Headstones were stolen by locals for practical use. Some were pushed over and broken to pieces out of hate, disrespecting not only the Jews who lived, but also those who were already dead. The headstone to Lena's mother's grave was broken and pushed off center. Lena wiped off the dirt, pulled the dried weeds that coiled around it as if trying to protect the stone, and placed a small smooth pebble on the part that remained standing, as was the custom.

"Mame," she whispered, "I am heartbroken for losing you while you were so young and vibrant, but I am comforted by the knowledge that you didn't witness the horrors that followed your death."

She proceeded to walk to the outskirts of town, locating a wooded area where, according to the accounts of the townspeople, her father and 95 other Jewish men, women, and children were buried in a deep pit. She reached a grove of fir trees, sat down, and leaned against a tall tree trunk. The site was pristine. The sound of a nearby brook completed the idyllic atmosphere. Birds chirped and hopped from branch to branch.

"Strange world," mused Lena. "No one can tell today what atrocities were carried out here. The earth seems so vibrant and rich, as if nurtured by the blood that was spilled here. Nature seems to want to cover it all up, to allow life to go on. Tate," she whispered, "I would give anything to see your face now and hear your voice. I came to pay my last respects to your memory. I am so sorry you had to die such a shameful death alone. *Yehi Zichro Baruch" (May his memory be a blessing)*, she prayed, uttering her father's name quietly, wiping a lone tear trailing down her cheek.

46

We thought the war killed you all

As the war approached its end, the Nazis attempted to obliterate all evidence of the death camps. They destroyed the structures, burned the corpses, and took the survivors on a death march to Germany, planning to use them as slave labor in their underground factories. Killing them in the gas chambers was not a viable solution anymore. Time wouldn't allow it. The Allied forces were advancing. The removal of the survivors had to be done in haste. More than half perished during the march.

For millions of survivors, the war did not end in September 1945. Eleven million remained displaced. They were expected to return to their countries of origin. For most, that was not a valid option. The homes they had fled from, or were forced to vacate when taken to concentration camps or pushed into constricted ghettos, were destroyed, looted, or taken over by their neighbors or by strangers.

The first thought of the liberated was to go home and see if their families had survived; they hitched rides, took trains, and walked hundreds of miles. Upon returning to their hometowns, the story was always the same: their family homes were occupied by strangers. On the doorstep stood a Pole, a Ukrainian, or a Latvian. The answer to their inquiries was always the same: "You don't live here anymore. There is no place for you. We thought the war killed you all."

The locals took their homes, apartments, fields, stores, and farms. Art objects were looted by their neighbors or confiscated by the Germans. Their countries of origin betrayed them and aided in their annihilation. For some, these were not countries they wished to go back to and rebuild a future.

Most of the world, including the United States, was reluctant to aid in the resettling of the Jewish refugees. They were considered subversive, communists, rebels, troublemakers. This was a lie Hitler had told the world repeatedly, that the Jews were a biological poison and a trouble-making people. With the spread of Russian rule and oppression, the Western world was worried. Communism became a nasty word.

Millions of displaced Jews, unwanted and rejected by European countries and the United States, now wandered, homeless and without a country, like the ancient tribes in the desert. They faced a world without compassion or care.

The Jewish people recognized that the only place they were going to be welcome and safe was their ancient homeland, Israel.

Most survivors experienced trauma and serious health conditions because of what they had endured. Many suffered from psychological difficulties and were often distrustful and apprehensive of authorities.

Bricha (Escape) was a Jewish partisan organization formed at the end of the war. Its aim was to provide aid to those who wished to escape the iron grip of the Soviets. The plan was to cross the borders into Germany, Austria, or Italy, now under Allied control, escaping the countries Russia had annexed during the war—the irony being that countries that had been intent on the annihilation of the Jews became their haven. Those who were unable or unwilling to return to their homes were directed to refugee camps, built for that purpose in those countries. Some 850,000 people were resettled by the occupying forces. These camps were referred to as "displaced persons camps," temporary facilities intended primarily for refugees from Eastern Europe and survivors of the Nazi concentration camps.

The survivors in those camps showed an amazing resilience, creating autonomous states where they kept alive their traditions and culture, waiting to be resettled while keeping some notion of a nation. Various ethnic and religious groups tended to concentrate in their own specific camps, where they quickly set up churches, synagogues, and schools.

The exodus, the illegal *Aliyah (immigration)* to Israel, began in 1946, aided by Mossad, a branch of the *Haganah* (Defense) underground—the pre-independence army of Palestinian Jews that brought in illegal immigrants.

Tens of thousands of survivors, transported out of the camps, were heading towards Palestine with the intention of entering it illegally by any means they could.

47

Communism became known as the iron curtain

A group of survivors, some young and others not so young, formed around Lena and Ama. They started making plans for the next leg of their journey to a time and a place that would offer them a peaceful existence.

Yakov appointed himself as the leader of the group. His size lent him an imposing air. The rest of the group were happy to go along. Following instructions seemed easier than initiating them. They were only too pleased to let someone else do the planning and the leading.

Yakov was an energetic man in his thirties. He had escaped the Nazis' roundup of the Jews.

In his hometown, Sigulda, he was known as "Yakov, the ladies' man." Because he was large and strongly built, many Latvian maidens secretly coveted his attention. Yakov's father was a tailor, mild mannered and gentle. He seemed to be liked by his neighbors and customers. Yakov's mother kept a strict Jewish home. His two younger sisters were as handsome as their brother and caught the eyes of the gentile youth. Yakov was extremely protective of his sisters and kept a watchful eye on their social affairs.

The unfortunate June morning when the Jews of Sigulda were hastily chased out of their homes by the German occupiers and rounded up for transport, Yakov happened to have spent the night with one of the maidens he used to bestow his favors upon. When night fell, Yakov sneaked back to his parents' home. He found it empty. The place had been ransacked and looted. A couple of stray chickens strutted around the yard, clucking in loud protest. None of the neighbors could tell him where his family had been taken. Talking to people he had known and trusted since birth, his family's neighbors and friends, he saw that they cast their eyes down. They were avoiding his questions, to which no one seemed to have answers. He spent his last night in the house he was born in. When dawn arrived, he gathered a few items left after the looting, packed his backpack, and headed out.

Yakov ended up spending the war years in hiding. The maiden who had saved his life by spending that fateful night with him hid him in the attic of her modest cottage. He never saw his parents or his sisters again. Documents he discovered after the war attested to them being taken to Kaiserwald, a concentration camp near Riga. Very few survived that place.

The group decided to head south. The plan was to cross the border into Lithuania and proceed into Poland. All movement between the different states annexed by Russia was closely monitored by heavily secured posts along each border.

Stalin's reign was ruthless. Communism became known as the iron curtain. After being liberated from the Nazi occupation, the conquered states were ruled by Communist puppet governments.

The group's destination was Munich, Germany. The country that had been intent on annihilating their race was now the place where they were about to find refuge. The route was planned by the *Bricha (escape)*, a select group of people with special talents. Ilka was part of this group. Their task was to furnish the refugees with false documents, planned routes, and contacts along the way.

It was winter, not a great time for trekking outdoors, but possibly a preferable time for stealing across borders. The cold weather forced the guards to huddle in their makeshift guard shacks rather than comb the area for possible escapees.

It was February. Ama had just turned five. They celebrated her birthday the night before their departure. Ilka and a couple of friends joined them for a meal and a small cake Lena managed to bake, even though butter and sugar were scarce commodities. Ilka lifted Ama while she was seated on a chair. He lifted her five times, for her five birth years, while the others counted and cheered, wishing her many years of joy, peace, and freedom. Ilka handed Ama a doll to keep her company on their travels. He held her tight and, again, promised that they would reunite very soon. Ama gave him a skeptical stare and looked down at her feet. She was getting tired of promises that the adults in her life, those she loved and missed so much, didn't seem to be able to keep.

Ama was the only child in a group of twelve. Some of them were middle aged. Walking many miles with weight on their backs or carrying suitcases was challenging, especially in cold weather.

Crossing into Lithuania was their first challenge. Stalin was ruthless about movement between the occupied states unless it was ordered by him, and those people were heading to work camps.

After traveling by train all night, the group was deposited in a small town near the Lithuanian border. It was early morning. There were few people to witness the arrival of the strange group, carrying their belongings, searching their surroundings in apparent confusion. The rain was relentless. The skies were grey. The weather matched their mood. They felt apprehensive about what lay ahead.

Lena wore her seal fur coat given to her by her father before she left home. As she headed towards an unknown future, it kept her warm. Ama was wrapped up in a woolen coat and high-top boots they had purchased for the trip. She held on to the doll Ilka gave her. She called her Baba, which means sorceress in Russian. She believed that magic was partly responsible for the reason she and her mother had survived the last five years. She often conversed with the unseen, inviting supernatural powers into her life, a life full of unpredictable dangers. It gave her a sense of security, easing her feelings of fear and uncertainty. She whispered comforting words into the doll's ears and hugged her tightly. She was too young to comprehend the details of their circumstances, and she knew not to ask too many questions. She had learned how to be quiet.

The address they were given led them to a deserted road. They marched in a procession, following in each other's footsteps. A small, empty wooden hut was their refuge for the day. It had mud floors and no windows. They had to wait for nightfall to resume their progress, a safer choice. Near the border, there were guard posts placed every few miles. Anyone traveling by foot or carriage in the direction of the border was halted. Their plan was to cross the border in the middle of the cold night, hoping that the guards would be huddled in their posts, well away from the freezing outdoors.

They settled along the walls of the small hut and sat or lay down on their spread coats, trying to rest before nightfall. A storm was brewing outside; the wind was fierce. They could hear the old wooden structure creaking around them. Some food brought from home was unpacked and shared. They spoke in low voices, listening intently for any sound approaching their hideaway. Lena, tired from the night's ride, dozed off.

Ama remained wide awake. Staring at the sleeping adults huddled along the walls, she was bored and looked for a means to entertain herself. A metal bed frame in the corner of the large room attracted her attention. There were bars across the bed, joined to the outer frame. She quickly found a new game. She grabbed the cross bars and started to do somersaults. A crash and a piercing cry woke Lena. Ama lay on the floor holding her head. It was a bad time to get hurt. There was no way to reach any medical facility. Lena held Ama, who moaned with pain. The familiar pain in her head intensified. Lena watched her closely, praying that it would not turn out to be a serious injury.

Gita, one of the older members of the group, stared at the young mother and her ailing child. She saw the distress on Lena's face. "I am a nurse," she whispered, as she approached Lena. "Let me look at her." Gita examined Ama's reactions and looked into her eyes. "She will be fine," she assured Lena. "There is no sign of concussion. Keep her warm and hydrated." She smiled at Lena and squeezed her arm in reassurance.

Gita had lost her husband and son in Kaiserwald, the largest Nazi concentration camp near Riga. The two men were grabbed at their place of work, a print shop they owned in the downtown area. Gita, aware of the rounding up of Jews that day, didn't return to her home. A Latvian family, friends of Gita and her husband, hid her in a farm home they owned in the countryside. She remained hidden for the duration of the war. Now, sitting on the mud floor, she pulled out photos from her rucksack and gazed at the images of her slain husband and son. She touched the photos to her lips and, with a sigh, tucked them back into her bag. Her only desire was to get to Israel and join the only family she had left, her sister and her brother-in-law, with hopes of picking up the remaining shreds of her life.

She looked towards the young woman rocking her daughter and felt a dull ache in her heart, remembering rocking her own son when he was a toddler.

The last rays of sun were disappearing below the horizon. Darkness settled over the room. The air was thick with anticipation. In a couple of hours, they were to embark on a dangerous trek towards the border.

48

"If she starts crying, I will strangle her"

Suspicious glances were thrown towards Lena and her daughter. "If she starts crying, I will strangle her," said Yakov, looking fiercely at Lena and Ama. He had the appearance of someone capable of keeping his word.

"You dare lay a finger on her, and I will kill you in your sleep," hissed Lena. She picked Ama up and tucked her under her coat.

Ama's little voice whispered a question: "Mama, is it okay if I breathe?"

The trek was long. They marched in a silent procession in the dark. A drizzle of light raindrops covered them in a damp blanket. The cold penetrated their clothing and chilled their bones. Yakov was in the lead, making sure their path was clear of obstacles, human or otherwise.

There were sounds of music and laughter in the distance. They could see lights through the branches of trees and brush. The sounds were coming from a camp of the Russian soldiers. The guards, off duty, were celebrating with vodka and music. The cold, damp air made most of them huddle close to their fires. No one wished to stray far from the camp.

The effort of walking in the rain and cold air started to show its effects. The older people in the group, tired and cold, began to cough. The sound alerted the border guards,

"*Stoy" (Stop)*! sounded a loud command, directed at the group. A uniformed guard appeared out of the brush and pointed his gun at them.

A couple of additional guards followed behind him. The first guard, who seemed to be in command, demanded to see their papers. After studying the produced documents, he glared suspiciously at the strange group.

His eyes fell on the child. He crouched down to her height, tousled her hair in mock fondness and motioned her to come closer. "Come here little girl," he crooned in a soft voice. He knew that a child might speak the truth, whatever it was. "Are you going on a nice trip?" he continued his interrogation. "Where is your home?"

Ama looked up at her mother, who smiled down at her and squeezed her shoulder in reassurance. She then returned her gaze to the soldier. He had a broad face covered with a thick fuzzy beard. He reminded her of a stray dog they had encountered on their travels. She remembered being eager to get close to the animal and sink her hand into its fur, but the sharp menacing teeth made her hesitant. She stared at the soldier's fuzzy beard and felt an urge to touch it. He was too close to her and smelled of stale tobacco and spirits. She decided that, like the dog, he was not to be trusted. She looked him straight in the eye without uttering a word. "Mama told you not to talk, right?" the guard continued in a sweet voice. He kept his fierce gaze on the child, hoping to shake her resolve.

"*Ana Balnaya" (She is ill)*, said Lena. "She is not right in the head," she added, gesturing to her temple. "She is deaf and dumb."

Ama liked the idea of being presented as deaf and dumb. It relieved her from having to answer anyone's annoying, confusing questions. She decided right there and then that this was who she would be from now on, or at least for the foreseeable future.

The guard stood up, scanned the group with his eyes, and motioned them to follow in his footsteps.

In the end, it was not the whimpering of a scared child that betrayed them. It was the sound of coughing and hacking by the adults.

49

She wasn't allowed to express her loss and sadness

The group was marched to a local county jail. They were placed in a large room with green concrete walls. The paint was peeling. The floor was hard-packed mud. There was no furniture. Light streamed through two small, barred windows.

"We will demand to see a high-ranking officer," said Yakov to his group, in an effort to sow some hope in their hearts. These small, out-of-the-way municipalities were known to carry out kangaroo trials which ignored law, justice, and due process. After a speedy, so-called trial, the defendants would be shipped to Siberia with a lifetime prison sentence. That was the better outcome. Execution by a firing squad was the other.

There was no place to rest your weight but the floor. Two small windows situated high on the wall, one facing the front of the building and one facing its back, were secured with metal bars. On the far side of the room, another small metal door suggested a way out towards the back of the building. They were to await the arrival of a high-ranking officer. He was coming the next morning to assess their case and decide their fate.

Ama was seated on the floor next to her mother. In her arms she clutched Baba, her magical doll. It was reassuring to hold a little magician in her arms. She had learned to rely on powers beyond the obvious at a very young age.

Lena was dozing off. Ama's eyes were darting from person to person. She heard the big man, Yakov, saying that he'd strangle her if she made any noise. She was determined to stay far away from him and be very quiet and not attract any unnecessary attention.

She stroked Baba's head and whispered in her ear. "The big bad man is not going to hurt you. I will protect you." Baba was the closest thing she had to a friend, and she confided in her, Sharing her secrets and fears. She wrapped the doll tightly in a soft blanket she carried and tucked her under her coat.

Baba's body was made of rags. The porcelain head was hollow. Inside Baba's head, Lena had hidden bills of money. This was Ilka's idea and probably one of the reasons he had acquired the doll. Undeclared amounts of money smuggled across borders was another sure way to end up in a Russian prison.

When the first rays of morning streamed through the bars of the windows, Lena, fearful that the money she hid in the doll's head would be discovered, made a decision. She had to get rid of the doll. She knew it would break little Ama's heart, but she didn't see any other way to avoid the discovery of the money. She bent down, looked at Ama, and softly told her that Baba needed to go outside, to get fresh air. Reluctantly Ama released her doll to her mother. Lena walked to the window that faced the back of the building and slid Baba through the bars. They heard it landing with a soft thump. Ama's eyes grew as big as saucers. Lena placed a finger across her lips signaling her daughter to remain quiet. Ama didn't understand why her doll was taken away from her, but she also knew that she wasn't allowed to express the loss and sadness she felt. She settled back on the floor and hung her head, hiding the tears trailing down her cheeks.

The rest of the forlorn group was waking up, coughing and groaning. Spending a night on a hard mud floor, using only their coats to keep the chill away, was difficult, especially for the aged among them.

A rumpled-looking older guard entered their cell with a samovar of hot tea and a few crude chipped cups. They sipped the tea in silence, taking turns using the few cups.

A commotion outside the window signaled the arrival of a dignitary. Rows of guards stood at attention. A man in an officer's uniform exited a military vehicle.

The group of prisoners clamored near the one small window, which was too small to encompass the scene in front of the building. They couldn't discern the reason for the commotion. They were all on high alert, fearing that the worst was yet to come.

The door to their cell opened shortly after. Two guards entered the room and placed a desk and a chair in the center. A tall dark-haired man in his fifties walked into the cell. His face didn't reveal any emotion. The shiny medals decorating the front of his impeccable uniform attested to his high rank. He waved his hand, motioning the guards to leave the room. He strode towards the one door at the end of the room, pulled a key from his pocket, unlocked it, then walked back and slowly lowered himself onto the one chair in the room.

His piercing dark eyes landed on each one of them in turn. No one spoke. In their minds, they all knew that this was probably the end of their hopeful journey. The best-case scenario would have them heading to Siberia to a work camp, where, if not the work, then the treacherous weather would finish them off. The worse one would place them in front of a firing squad with no further investigation.

His gaze lingered on the little girl peeking out from behind her mother's legs. "*Idzi suda*" (Come here), he said in a soft voice, motioning to her with his finger. Ama raised her eyes to her mother. Lena gave her daughter a gentle push, directing her to approach the officer. Life for Ama was full of questions and riddles. She had to rely on the adults in her life, mainly her mother, to direct her in making wise, safe decisions. She took the cue from her mother and hesitantly walked towards the man in the chair. The officer looked at the little girl and stroked her hair. He gently raised her chin to meet her eyes. "Are you hungry?" he asked in a soft voice. Ama nodded her head and replied that she was. He reached in his pocket and pulled out a small bar of chocolate. He handed it to the child and motioned her to go back and stand near her mother.

"You are a bunch of Jews, aren't you?" he directed his words to the group. "You were caught because you were attempting to cross the border, which is against the law, right? I'll tell you what," he continued, "you see that door in the corner of this room? It is unlocked, open it, get out and run as fast as you can towards the woods in the back of this building. Don't look back and don't stop." He gave them one last look, got up and abruptly left the room.

This was a known ploy, intended to efficiently get rid of prisoners. Shooting fleeing prisoners would not be questioned by the authorities. There would be no investigation. The group knew what was awaiting them outside this building. No trial, no Siberian prison, just a quick and tidy execution.

They weren't left with many choices but to obey and leave the cell. Lena placed the backpack on her shoulders and picked up Ama. She tucked her under her coat and was the first to open the unlocked door and burst outside. She ran down the hill not looking back. Ama did look back at the building. She saw Baba lying next to the building's wall. She wished she could run back and pick her up. The memory of her beloved doll, abandoned, lying face down on the muddy ground would remain in her memory for years to come.

There were no shots. The air was still. The 400 meters to the edge of the woods seemed to stretch forever. The few minutes it took to reach safety, where the trees would obscure them from view, seemed like an eternity. Lena reached the edge of the woods and fell to her knees under a tree, trying to catch her breath. The rest of the group followed. They all survived. No one attempted to stop them or shoot them. They looked at each other, dumbfounded. Their faces showed relief and confusion.

"He was a Jew," exclaimed one of the group.

"I knew it," muttered Yakov. Some Jewish men, disguised as Russians, managed to infiltrate the military and climb up to high ranks. The belief that their lives were spared thanks to one of their own brought the disheveled group joy and pride.

50

"These are partisans," whispered Yakov. "We are safe"

The tired group wondered cluelessly for the next five hours. It was getting close to nightfall. They were hoping to reach civilization and inquire about their whereabouts and the proximity to the border.

Lena carried Ama on her back. The long hours of trekking were too much for Ama's Little legs. Sarah, a gentle soul Lena had befriended, offered to carry her backpack. Lena's whole body was aching, demanding rest. She knew that she could not stray away from the group. She had to keep pace with them. Her and her daughter's survival depended on it.

On one of their rest stops, Lena unwrapped the last small package of food she had from her pack, took out a couple of wheat cakes slathered with the leftover honey she carried in a small jar, and shared them with her little daughter. Ama, who had remained quiet through long hours of hunger, devoured the food eagerly.

Close to where they settled to rest, Lena noticed bushes, their branches heavy with ripe blackberries. The taste of the berries revived her spirit. Yakov gave a signal that it was time to continue their journey. Lena wiped Ama's juice-stained face and got ready to join the rest of the group.

"Who goes there?" came a loud voice from deep in the thick woods. Yakov signaled the group to stop. "Better show yourselves, we are armed," commanded a stern voice. "These are partisans," whispered Yakov. "We are safe."

Approximately 30,000 Jews became irregular fighters. Many of them were teenagers, men, and women. The majority were regular folks who had escaped the ghettos and work camps. They joined organized resistance groups that were fighting the Nazis. They hid in forests and the urban underground, constantly moving in the shadows on the edges of cities and towns. Most of them knew nothing about guns and ammunition and had no military training. Some came with families that were hidden in enclaves deep in the forests.

They took part in the underground press distribution of leaflets calling for rebellion and resistance. They played a significant role in the Allied invasion of Normandy in 1944, blowing up railway lines, attacking trains, and hindering Germany's ability to mount a quick defense.

The Partisans were instrumental in assisting Jews to get to safe havens, helping them cross borders into friendly countries and escape to Palestine. Lena and her group had landed in safe hands.

The group hesitantly approached the armed men. Ama hid behind her mother, not knowing if the guns were going to hurt her. A young girl separated from the group. She approached Ama and extended her arms. "You are safe, Malyutka" (little one), she said to Ama. "My name is Lidia. I am a friend." Her warm brown eyes and big smile were disarming. Slowly Ama came out of her hiding place behind Lena's legs. She melted into Lidia's embrace.

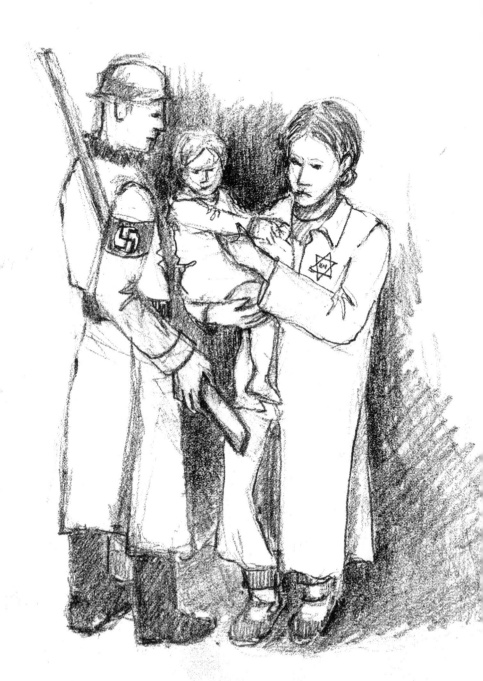

51

They were shoved and packed into the car like sardines

Lidia was sixteen. She joined the partisans when she was fourteen. She and her mother traveled from place to place, escaping the long tentacles of the German authorities. Their story of survival was of epic proportions. They came from Czechoslovakia. Their small town, in the Carpathian Mountains, was invaded and occupied by Nazi Germany in March 1939. The Jews were deported to the Theresienstadt Ghetto, north of Prague. About 33,000 died from the camp's harsh conditions, mostly from starvation. The survivors were sent to Auschwitz.

The train ride took many hours. The car had no windows and no ventilation. The vast number of people stuffed in each car allowed only standing room. The weak and elderly crouched by the car's walls. Others offered them water and soft clothing for comfort.

Lidia and her mother huddled in a corner holding on to each other. Lidia's eyes fell on a young mother, standing next to them. She was holding an infant under her jacket. A small boy, just a toddler, clutched her skirt. She would stroke his hair from time to time but soon had to return her attention to the infant.

"What's your name?" whispered Lidia, inching towards the boy.

"Ezra," answered the boy in a thin high voice.

"Are you scared, sweetheart?" She continued engaging the boy in a conversation. A vigorous head movement came as an answer. Yes, he was scared and confused. He had been torn away from his father's arms at the station. His father had tried to resist being separated from his family. The last scene Ezra saw was his father, lying on the ground, bleeding, beaten with the butt of a soldier's rifle. He heard his mother's heart-wrenching sobs, and the next thing he knew he was roughly picked up and thrown into the open door of the train's car. So, yes, he was scared, traumatized and confused. He was only four years old. Not much of what had happened made any sense to him, and none of the adults were available for explanations.

Lidia crouched down to his height, reached into her coat pocket, and pulled out a small candy. "Here," she said, "try this. It might make you feel better. Okay?" Ezra gave her a hesitant smile. A small sparkle returned to his dark brown eyes. He stepped forward and hugged this strange girl who had reached out to him in this time of confusion.

The train ride, shoved and packed into the car like sardines, was harrowing. Lidia's mother hovered over her fourteen-year-old daughter, protecting her from being trampled. Fear and desperation, at times, made people forget their humanity, considering only their own survival. Lidia was large for her age and strongly built, which helped her survive the long ride.

52

"ARBEIT MACHT FREI"

ARBEIT MACHT FREI (WORK SETS YOU FREE). These large, illuminated letters were inscribed above a gate leading into a camp, supposedly designed as a work camp. Lively march music was sounding from loudspeakers. Gay music, celebratory music. Music intended to lift and calm people's spirits and deflect their attention from the plumes of smoke and strange burning smell coming out of an ominous grey building.

They arrived late. It was dark outside. Upon entering the gates of the camp, the men were ordered to step away from the women and were marched to an undisclosed location. Lidia never saw her father again after that night. She saw the young mother and her two children ushered away into a different building.

The large room she and her mother were pushed into together with other women, was bathed in a piercing artificial light. They were ordered to strip. They were left hovering in the corners of the room attempting to cover their nakedness. Lidia stood behind her mother. She was the only teen girl in the room. Two soldiers stood guard next to the building's door. There was a sense of dread. A smell of fear and perspiration permeated the room.

An impeccably dressed officer entered. He had blue piercing eyes and a voice that sounded like splintered ice. In a hand that was clad in a white leather glove, he held a crop. He stopped in front of the frightened group and smiled.

"Welcome to our work camp," he declared. "After an initial inspection and evaluation of your abilities you will be assigned to the different posts and directed to your barracks." He stopped, flicking an invisible crumb off his perfectly pressed sleeve, and started a slow pace of the room, eying each woman in turn, his gaze lingering on them while he pointed and probed different parts of their bodies with his crop. The atmosphere was reminiscent of a cattle market. He noticed the girl hiding behind her mother's body. "Come out, little one," he motioned to her. "Let's have a look at you." He approached Lidia slowly. She could smell his scent, foul and sweet like flowers on a grave. "Yes, you are a young thing, aren't you? How old are you?" Lidia couldn't find her voice. "Speak up," he ordered in a menacing tone.

"Fourteen," answered Lidia.

His eyes fell on her full young breasts. He smiled and said, "Why don't you go and stand over there with the younger women? We'll decide what to do with you later." He kept ordering and pointing his crop left and right, directing them to move to their assigned spots, deciding who had a chance for a meager future and whose life he was ending with one motion of his arm.

This apparition, only vaguely resembling a human, was Josef Mengele, "The Angel of Death." He oversaw the selection of incoming prisoners for either torturous labor or immediate extermination, shouting left or right to direct them to their fate. Eager to advance his medical career, he began experimenting on live Jewish prisoners in the guise of deadly medical "treatments."

Loud sirens pierced the air, signaling danger to alert the camp's officers. At times the signal meant that a riot had broken out among the prisoners or that someone had attempted escape. The room where the women were kept erupted into chaos. They attempted to flee the building. Mengele ordered them to be locked in the barracks.

The officers started hitting the women with the butts of their rifles, attempting to take control of the situation. Lidia grabbed her mother by her arm, and they pushed their way through the mayhem. She grabbed a couple of army coats hanging on pegs next to a back exit, threw one on her mother's shoulders and wrapped herself in the other. She pushed against the emergency exit. The opening of the emergency door activated an alert, but its sound was drowned in the piercing noise of the emergency siren. All the soldiers' attention was directed to the source of the problem created by a group of inmates who were trying to climb over the barbed-wire fence. They were all gunned down. The rest of the prisoners were herded towards the barracks and locked inside.

The attention of the guards situated on the tall towers was on the unfolding drama within the camp. Lidia and her mother slipped quietly through a large gap left in the barbed wire fence. Running across the barren field that surrounded the camp, they reached the woods and disappeared into the night. After several excruciating miles, walking barefoot and huddling naked under the German officers' rough coats, they encountered a group of partisans and fell into their rescuing arms.

Lidia, a resourceful fourteen-year-old, had saved herself and her mother from imprisonment or execution. Ama was elated to find a friend and a companion. In Lidia she had found her match. She adored Lidia and, despite the age difference, the two became inseparable.

Lena and her group were fortunate. They now had armed, strong, determined young people accompanying them on their travels through Poland.

53

Lifeless human forms were dangling from the trees

They were headed to Vilna, moving at night, staying away from the watchful eyes of the Russian border patrols. It was early morning. Ama woke up next to her mother. They were camped out in the woods next to a small rural village near the Polish border. The camp was quiet. People were moving about, tending small fires on which they prepared their makeshift meals. Lena noticed that several of the partisans were missing. Yakov was among them. He had attached himself to their group with apparent admiration.

After setting up camp, a group of the partisans would often mysteriously disappear, their rifles perched on their shoulders, their faces stern. They would return to camp late at night, silent and distant, as if guarding a secret.

After morning chores were done, the group got organized and continued their travels towards the border. They walked through the woods, closely following David, a man who appeared to be the partisans' leader. The mood was somber. Lidia held Ama's hand and softly reassured her of their safety. Ama's eyes fell upon a strange shadow on the ground, approaching a bend in the path. She gave a small shriek that alerted the attention of the adults. Five lifeless human forms were dangling from the trees, ropes tied around their necks. Their vacant eyes seemed to stare at the group, some with apparent surprise and others showing their final agony. Each had a note pinned to their body with the word *"NAKAM" (AVENGE)* printed in large, bold black letters.

The partisans Lena's group had joined were part of a movement, formed at the end of the war. *Nakam (avenge in Hebrew)* was a group of young men and women, survivors of the Holocaust, who fought in the resistance, seeking revenge against their former tormentors. The message became a rallying cry for the newborn state of Israel, declaring that the days when attacks on Jews went unanswered were over. "Never Again" became the prevailing mantra. They could not let the crimes against their people go unpunished. Their aim was to exact revenge.

"We are proud of you all for planning to join our people in Palestine and help rebuild our homeland," said David, addressing Lena's group. "There is still unfinished business here, in the diaspora. Those who were intent on annihilating us need to answer for their crimes. We need to avenge our slain brothers and sisters."

Most holocaust survivors were too weary or devastated after their world was shattered to think about revenge. For many, merely rebuilding their lives and starting new families was revenge enough against a Nazi regime that aimed to destroy them. Others believed that physical retribution ran counter to Jewish morals and traditions. The concept of reprisals seemed pointless, given the sheer scope of the genocide.

The Nuremberg trials were intended to prosecute the top Nazis, but there was no Jewish representation in the proceedings. Many young people felt a deep sense of injustice, witnessing most Nazis reintegrate themselves back into the European population, staying in hiding, fearing reprisals.

The plan of the *Nakam* group was simple: "kill Germans, as many as possible," targeting the worst Nazi perpetrators. Yakov had found his mission. The *Nakam* group spoke to his sense of final justice.

54

If you do this for me, God,
I promise to be a very good girl

Vilna is situated in southeastern Lithuania. It shares a border with Poland. During the Nazi occupation, the Jews of Vilna were moved to one of the largest ghettos in Europe. Food, water, medical supplies, and other necessities were withheld from them by the Nazis. Sanitary living was made virtually impossible.

Living in ghettos resulted in segregation, humiliation, and ultimately death. It was designed to ruin people's health, human dignity and, ultimately, their lives.

Lena's group reached Vilna, barely escaping imprisonment by the KGB. Their plan was to cross into Poland and steal their way across the country into German territory, a place where they wouldn't have to fear Russian persecution. Yakov, the one with a raging, restless soul, stayed behind and joined the avenging partisans.

Germany, a country that was responsible for murdering six million of their people, ironically was now designated, by the Allied forces, as a place of refuge for those that survived the persecution. Crossing from Poland to Germany was the last dangerous challenge they faced.

Dani was a young, charismatic man. He was close to the Bricha organization and was sent from Palestine to help with the placement of Jewish survivors. The group met him in a small suburb of Vilna near the Polish border.

"I am here to help you plan the rest of your trip and make sure that you end up in a place where you will feel safe," he said to Lena's group. The instructions they were given were precise. Again, they were to hide in a deserted building near the railway lines and wait for nightfall, at which time he would come and inform them of the details of their trip.

A small, rickety structure loomed in the fading light. They reached it at sunset, after what seemed like a very long walk from the train station, arriving from Vilna. They had a few hours to rest and regroup. Ama huddled close to her mother. She reached into the small backpack she carried and pulled out her small, worn blanket. It was a poor replacement for her trusted companion, Baba. She looked up at Lena's face. Her mother was dozing off. That morning she had awakened stiff and sore. The long hours scrubbing floors on her hands and knees at the officers' cabinet in Ufa were taking their toll.

Precisely at midnight, Dani came to lead them to their next destination. The inky sky stretched above. Darkness covered them like a soft blanket. It seemed that even the stars dimmed their glow in an effort to hide and ensure the travelers' safety. They arrived back at the train station. The place was quiet and deserted. A lonely watchman was sitting inside the station, his head slumped on his chest, deep asleep.

They found themselves standing in front of seven still, black trains looming in the dark. The group huddled around Dani, who, in a soft whisper, described to them what the next leg of their journey entailed. "You are to crawl under the seven trains and arrive on the other side of the tracks. There you will find a cargo train. One of the cars will have an unlocked door. That's the car you will travel in for the duration of your trip."

The train was en route to Poland. One car, empty of any passenger amenities, was allocated for the eleven refugees. It had been procured through an exorbitant bribe to the local train authorities.

The task ahead seemed quite impossible. Part of the group was inflicted with aches and limited physical abilities. The stronger, younger people relieved them of their belongings to allow them freedom of movement while crawling under the trains.

Ama was silent. She sat on the ground, holding on to her mother's coattail. Her knowledge of what awaited ahead was limited. There was no time for lengthy explanations. She assessed her situation and was resigned to the fact that, as scary as it seemed, she had to follow and do what she was told. She saw seven still train cars in front of her and was told to crawl under them and cross to the other side. A clenching fear grabbed hold of her. She was afraid that one of those trains would start moving while she was beneath it.

Ama's first five years were not a typical childhood. There were no bedtime stories, questions about the universe, or pondering the existence of a higher power. The answers to these initial childhood thoughts came, mostly, from within herself. Bewildered, she turned to a higher power, on which she learned to rely in times of need, to come to her aid and rescue.

"God," She whispered, looking up at the sky, "Don't let any of those scary trains start moving while I am underneath them. If you do this for me God, I promise to be a very good girl and obey everything that is asked of me." She also learned to bargain at a young age.

In a flash she decided that she was not going to stick with her mother and the group. They were way too slow in their moves. She was only concerned about her own survival, and, at that moment, she wasn't sure how much she could trust the adults to keep her safe. She sprinted ahead and, like a small animal, crawled under the seven cars at a lizard's quick pace.

Lena found her daughter on the other side, sitting on the ground, a big, shining bruise developing on her forehead above one eye. Moving with speed, she had been hit by a protruding part under one of the trains.

55

She would never suffer from thirst again

The train car that was to transport them across the Polish border was devoid of windows. It was a wooden enclosure with only one large opening with sliding doors to get in or out. It was a cattle train, which didn't offer the passenger any means of comfort. Lena's group settled against the walls of the car. Some were leaning on their packs, some were lying down on their spread coats. They were ready to endure a twenty-hour ride across Poland, crossing a thousand miles into Germany that now was under the control of the Allied forces. Crossing that border would finally get them away from the Russian grip and ensure their safety.

"This is a crazy world," mused Lena. "We are heading to the country whose people were intent on eliminating my people. A country from which I was running away and hiding for the last five years. Now this country is where our people are to find refuge and safety. Unbelievable."

Ama was not informed of the journey's plan and its fine details. She settled against her mother, holding on to a small worn-out blanket that had brought her some comfort after Baba was taken away from her. She didn't know if being locked up in this windowless, barren enclosure was going to last a day or a week, and she had learned not to ask too many questions. She knew the other people in the group, but, besides Luba, the nurse, who had helped Lena after Ama's fall, none seemed friendly. Times of crisis brought out opposite sides in people. There were those who couldn't elevate themselves above caring only for their own personal needs and survival, and those who maintained the capability of lending a helping hand in times of need. Lena's group was comprised mainly of middle-aged adults. They were sunk deep in their own existence and the best way to preserve it.

The rhythmic sound of the train rushing over the tracks lulled the people to sleep. Lena gave in to the fatigue that plagued her most of her waking hours. She lay down on her coat and fell into a deep sleep.

Ama, bored and restless, stretched out on her stomach and peered through the cracks of the broken boards on the sides of the car. She could see streaks of passing green fields and forests and quaint little farms with red roofs and smoking chimneys, a connection to an idyllic world, a world that she was not a part of. It existed outside, while she was locked up in this dark, stuffy wooden box. She became lethargic and fell asleep next to her mother.

Lena dreamed. All her cares and worries fell away. All her pains as well. She was laughing and dancing. Ilia and Micha approached her with bright smiles and open arms. She was on the verge of feeling their arms reach out and embrace her when a sharp jolt woke her up.

The rest of the car's occupants were awake and alert too. The train had stopped. There was a commotion outside their car. They had reached a checkpoint and had been stopped for inspection. Outside they heard Russian commands in loud voices.

"Mama, are they going to take us away?" whispered Ama. "Will they take me away from you?" she continued in a small, fearful voice, holding her tears back.

"Never," hissed Lena. She took Ama under her arm and covered her with the small blanket she carried.

There was banging on the cars' walls and the voices got closer. The footsteps stopped by the door to their car. Slowly and deliberately, the wide door slid open. The man that peered at them from the opening was clad in a Russian uniform. He was tall and carried a fair amount of weight. He stared into the car. The silence was ear piercing, as if by keeping silent the people in the car thought they would become invisible. He moved his eyes from one face to another until his gaze fell on the small child peeking from under her mother's embracing arm. The child's eyes spoke of hunger, thirst, fear, and resignation. He kept his eyes on the child for a long time and slowly slid the door shut.

"*Prodolzhay*" *(Keep going),* came a loud command, and, with a bang on the car's wall, they felt the train slowly accelerating ahead, onward to their destination.

The sparse rations of food and water had weakened Ama. She lay down, quiet and listless. The train came to a sudden halt in a middle of a wheat field. The heavy doors slid open with a creaking sound. The bright sunlight streaming into the car blinded the passengers after a long ride in darkness. Everyone was jumping off into the light, stretching their limbs and turning their faces towards the sun. In the middle of the field, they saw a hand water pump. Vessels and containers appeared. People were running towards the pump and standing in line. They filled a large bucket with water and kept dipping metal cups, filling them with the reviving liquid and quenching their thirst. Ama cast her eyes into the depth of the train car. In a far corner she saw an empty bottle rolling on its side. With the found bottle she approached the jovial group. She first drank from a cup with the others. After all the adults filled their containers and quenched their thirst, she dipped her bottle into the bucket and filled it with water. She promised herself that, if she could help it, she would never be thirsty again.

The group was sitting around, partaking of the life-giving liquid, enjoying the fresh air. Ama climbed into the train car and hid her treasure deep in a corner. The bottle did not have a cap. She placed it on its end, hiding it near her mother's belongings.

One of the adults noticed her actions. He shared it with the others, who found it amusing. It caused the people to laugh and look in her direction, which deeply shamed her. She felt ridiculed, when it probably was just gentle amusement at her ingenuity.

56

Is her hand going to be black because he is holding it?

Noi Freyman (New freeman) was a small, gated quarter in central Munich. It was the displaced persons camp Lena and Ama were assigned to. It consisted of wooden structures, hastily built as temporary homes for those who had survived the war. Most of them were Jewish.

The United Nations Relief and Rehabilitation's (UNRRA) mission was to provide economic assistance to European nations at the end of the war and to repatriate and assist the refugees who were liberated by the Allied forces.

Upon arrival, the people and their belongings had to go through a delousing process. Their clothes came back at the other end, compressed into a small package, covered with a white silvery dust.

Ama was given a long, new coat. It was navy blue with two rows of brass buttons. A pair of new high-top black boots completed the ensemble. There was no prouder little person than she, marching around in her newly acquired attire.

Lena and Ama were assigned to a two-story wooden structure. They shared their new home with a couple and their baby. They were given a one-room apartment on the second floor. They shared one bed. A table that stood in the middle of the room served for meals and all other activities. A shared kitchen on the lower floor was used by both families for meal preparations. Lena did her best to create a cozy home for herself and her daughter. She rediscovered her aesthetic sense. An exquisitely embroidered tablecloth adorned their table to greet the Shabbat. A small vase with wildflowers always adorned the center of the table. The turmoil of the last five years started to fade. It all seemed like a bad dream. She was young and resilient. Life started to feel normal again. Lena dared to exhale and feel hope for a brighter future.

Ilka was a frequent visitor to their small home. They celebrated his visits with special meals Lena prepared by getting the best ingredients she could afford from the local store to make a simple but tasty meal for the three of them. His sparkling personality, humor, and talent for storytelling kept them riveted.

Ama adored her handsome uncle. She would climb onto his lap and stroke his face. "Why don't you come stay with us?" she inquired. "We can make a sleeping space for you the way we did in Ufa. I really miss you when you are gone," she added.

"We will all be together very soon, Amichka" he answered, stroking her fine hair. "I have very important work to do first. This work will help you and your mama go to Israel, where your uncles and cousins are waiting for you."

"Well," said Ama after considering his answer, "then read this book to me. I am starting to learn how to read but I am still very slow." She shared with him the latest books she was working on in the makeshift kindergarten, created for the children of the camp. Ama was an animated girl and loved his participation and his attention to the happenings in her life, since, most of the time, her mother was too tired or preoccupied to pay attention.

Ilka was an essential part of the *Bricha (Escape)* organization that handled the needs of displaced people. They were finding ways to reunite those people with their families and help them travel to their chosen destinations by providing them with false documents. "It'll take about twelve months," he told his sister. "There are hundreds and thousands of people waiting to be sorted out. Be patient. Your turn will come. You will be heading to Palestine where you'll join our brothers. This is the family we have left. We must stick together. I will come when my work here is done, when every one of the survivors has been taken care of."

Lena settled into a waiting mode. There were courses offered in several occupations at the community center. Lena joined a group of women training to become seamstresses. Her interest was children's clothes.

On weekends, Lena and Ama, dressed in warm clothes, with Ama's hand tucked firmly into Lena's, strolled the streets of the war-ravaged city, trying to find corners that still attested to its former glory.

Ama's eyes darted across the new unfamiliar sites. The buildings, the lights, the loud city sounds, were all foreign to her. The first five years of her life she had spent slinking along the outskirts of civilization.

Walking on the sidewalk, her height caused her to notice people's lower backs and hands. She was mesmerized by the hands of African American soldiers holding on to the white hands of German girls. It was the first time she had encountered people from different races. "Is her hand going to be black because he is holding it?" She asked her mother, out of pure amazement and curiosity.

Lena found a local seamstress and ordered a few dresses for Ama and herself. The five years of being clothed in worn-out, not always clean, garments were behind her. Part of feeling human again included taking care of her appearance. Ama reveled in her new blue frock adorned with lines of ruffles on its bodice.

"You have such a tiny, cute nose," said Lena to her daughter, running her finger along Ama's profile. Lena's nose was handsome but prominent, with a bump in its middle.

Intimate close moments like this between mother and daughter were rare. Once the main task of motherhood, ensuring her offspring's survival, was achieved, it seemed like the need for closeness evaporated.

Lena embraced her daughter and kissed her gently on the cheek. This intimate gesture was the last time Ama remembered sharing a moment of affection with her mother. She was five years old.

57

She saw a group of people carrying a stretcher with a lifeless body

Berale was a six-year-old boy in Ama's class who captured her heart. He had an infectious smile and a mischievous way about him. She enjoyed watching him do stunts on the playground while the brown cap he always wore flew to the ground. He was always smiling in her direction, making sure that she was aware of each of his moves. He was so different from her, so free and daring, compared to the way she had learned to move through her life, always cautious.

They became close and spent many hours playing, immersed in a make-believe world. "Let's play mommy and daddy," suggested Berale, his big brown eyes twinkling with mischief. They were rummaging in an unfinished construction site on the outskirts of the compound.

"All right," answered Ama. "What shall we do?"

"Well," continued Berale. "You have to take your pants off and show me what you have down there," he pointed at her groin.

"You go first," she answered.

Berale considered the situation, stared at Ama for a moment and said, "Never mind, Let's go play hide and seek."

Munich was a significant cultural and industrial German city. During the war it had suffered seventy air raids, which left fifty percent of the city destroyed. The roads were packed with Allied army military vehicles, zooming here and there at a deadly speed. The prominent gate guarding the small refugee enclave kept its inhabitants secure and safe. Those venturing out needed to take extra care.

Lena warned Ama not to leave their camp unsupervised. She didn't need much convincing. Being cautious had become second nature to her.

Ama was playing in the backyard of her school when she heard a piercing wail followed by a commotion. She saw a group of people moving towards the school structure, carrying a stretcher with the lifeless body. A brown cap was peeking from under the cloth that covered the body. A sharp pain pierced Ama's insides. She ran breathless towards the school.

It was her sweet little friend. Berale. So typical of his nature, he had ventured outside the safety of the compound's gates. His adventurous spirit, seeking freedom, needed to explore, to break away from boundaries. He had been hit by a speeding army truck.

58

A large hand swiftly pulled his hand off Lena's shoulder

Marseille was the next stop for Lena and Ama before reaching Palestine's shores. It was a quaint French coastal town known as a crossroads for immigration and trade. Among the traded goods were drugs. As such it was not known as the safest city.

Due to its strategic location as a port, the city was fiercely fought over by both Germans and the Allied forces. It was liberated in the summer of 1944.

The port city recovered quickly; however, the dark influences of drug trafficking and prostitution returned, too. Gangs were fighting over controls of territories. The harbor, especially, loomed, dark and dangerous.

A small section of town, near the port, was allocated for displaced refugees who were waiting for their papers, mostly false, to allow them to board ships or further cross borders and enter foreign countries. Ilka was among the organizers, helping people with the necessary documents and contacts. His artistic skills helped in the actual creations of the various false documents.

Lena was given one bed for herself and Ama. They shared a large room with other women and children. The lack of privacy and constant chatter wore Lena down. There wasn't much to occupy herself with. It was a time to be patient and wait. An end to the nightmare was finally in sight. The wait became more and more challenging. She resorted to taking long walks by herself along the waterfront.

The sky was grey and a breeze caressed Lena's face, a welcomed coolness. She had escaped the constant chatter and stuffy air in the room she was sharing with 15 other women. The walk along the waterfront revived her. She was fatigued. The years of continuous running from one place to another had caught up with her. "I am so tired," she thought. "One day I will allow myself to be strong again but not today."

A group of French sailors, home on leave, were celebrating with the aid of an ample quantity of spirits. They noticed Lena and crossed the road, approaching her. "You're a pretty little dumpling," said one of the sailors. "Why don't you come with us and help us celebrate our freedom and our defeat of the Bosch?" Lena veered away and tried to cross to the other side of the road. "Not so fast, little one," said one of them. He placed one arm around her shoulder and pulled her close to him.

A large hand swiftly pulled his hand off Lena's shoulder, grabbed her by the arm, and pulled her away from the drunken sailors. It was a man from Lena's enclave who was also taking a solitary stroll along the city's port. He was very tall and strongly built. The sailors gave him the once over and retreated, swaying in their drunkenness.

"Thank you" muttered Lena. "I am glad you were nearby."

"Not a good idea to walk alone along this waterfront," said her rescuer. "Better to do it with a friend, the bigger the better," he added with a wink. "My name is Nathan. I would be glad to accompany you on your walks, for your protection of course," he added.

"Thank you" answered Lena. She casted her gaze down. Any new involvements with the opposite sex didn't interest her yet.

59

If you will it, it is no dream

Nathan was a handsome young man. With a full head of black curls and warm brown eyes, he attracted the attention of the females in the small settlement. Young women were interested in the young men, and the men reciprocated their attention. Six years of living in fear, concentrating mainly on ways to survive, had robbed them of six years of their young lives. The human spirit was resilient. They were waking up, responding to nature's call. Without the fear of survival hovering over their heads, people turned their attention to living, laughing, dreaming, and courting.

Nathan had been discharged from the Russian army when the war ended. Settling back in Poland, his country of origin, was not an option. No one in his family had survived the Nazi occupation. His parents, sister, and brother were among Hitler's earliest casualties. He had fled the country for Russia days before the Germans advanced on his town.

Nathan was heading to Palestine. He was determined to start a new life in a new young country. He was a follower of Theodor Herzl, the father of Zionism, whose teachings prompted a Jewish immigration to Palestine in an effort to form a Jewish state. Herzle's words, "If you will it, it is no dream," were carved in his mind. He was planning to take part in creating this future land for his people.

Lena, with her light blond hair and blue eyes, caught the attention of several young men, Nathan among them. Lena remained oblivious. Her survival pivoted on arriving in Palestine and joining her brothers.

Nathan gained an admirer, too. Little Ama was mesmerized by the tall dark man who so reminded her of the ones she had lost and missed. The admiration was mutual. Nathan loved spending time with the inquisitive little girl. They went on walks and had long talks about anything that occupied little Ama's interests.

"Do you like my mama?" she interrogated Nathan.

"Yes, I do," he replied,"

"Do you like her a lot?" she continued her questioning.

"Actually," he was talking in a whisper, "she doesn't know it, but I do like her a lot."

"So," punctuated Ama, gesturing with her little hands. "Why don't you tell her? We don't have a husband and we don't have a father. You will be perfect. I think you should tell her. I think she does like you too. She told me the other day, she said, 'You know Ama, Nathan is really a nice person.'" She winked at him with a self-satisfied look on her face. Her mission was accomplished. She knew what she wanted, and she was doing her best to make it happen.

A water pond, not too far from their habitation, was a place they frequented. Nathan would bring soap and create lots of lather and bubbles while washing Ama's hair. She reveled in the attention and frequently thought that maybe it was Nathan and she that were the match made in heaven.

The loving care Nathan showed to her child warmed Lena's feelings towards him. Her heart, toughened by years of fear and loneliness, started to soften. Nathan's gentle affection was like a healing balm to her soul.

"What are your plans when we arrive in Israel?" asked Nathan. They were walking in a nearby park holding hands. The strolling couple had to keep their guard up. The city streets, at dark, reeked of danger. Prostitutes offered their services in doorways, and shady exchanges took place on street corners.

"I will be joining my brothers' families." Said Lena. "They are part of two settlements along the Lake of Galilee." She looked up at Nathan, considering the possibility of their immanent parting. "Please let me know your whereabouts. I don't want us to lose contact with each other," she said.

Nathan squeezed her hand, raised it to his lips and gently kissed it. "I feel so lucky I found you. I will not let us drift apart."

60

Skinny people are not allowed to enter this country

Ilka told Lena that it would take three months for their turn to come to board a boat heading to Palestine.

A large central hall served as a dining room. They were served three simple meals a day. Food was suddenly available. Lena was determined to make up for years of deprivation. She coaxed her daughter to consume large quantities of food. Ama refused to cooperate. She was of slight build and not prone to large meals. This struggle between mother and daughter hovered over them for years to come. Ama always seemed too thin to her mother, and Lena continued to worry that the food her daughter consumed was not sufficient to sustain a healthy existence.

To appease her mother, Ama would wolf portions of her food standing up, ready to bolt, "If you eat standing up, you'll get fat legs," warned Lena. Meals, for Lena, became sacred events not to be missed or consumed in haste.

"What would happen if I ate sitting down?" wondered Ama. Ama grew into adulthood never needing large amounts of food; however, the fear of not having enough to eat when hunger struck remained with her for the rest of her life. Wherever she went as a child and as an adult she made sure to carry food with her, food that was rarely eaten but always stashed away in a pocket or a small bag, like the soft blanket a young child would drag around for comfort.

Lena told Ama about the wonderful country that awaited them. Ama couldn't wait to reach the shores of this wonderland. Everything in that place was going to be beautiful, the people, handsome and kind.

"Skinny people are not allowed to enter that country," said Lena to Ama. "You'd better finish your food and gain some weight before we get there."

Ama considered her mother's words, not sure how to approach this problem. She had always been thin. She wondered if she could make herself eat enough to change that.

The mail was not moving at an optimal pace during the war and the period after; however, Lena did get some correspondence from her brothers in Palestine. Lena's brother, Ari, sent Lena letters and photos of his family. In one of those photos, his eldest daughter, Tamar, was seen, holding a very large book with her very skinny arm draped across the cover. Ama studied the picture for a long time, looked at her mother, and asked: "How come she is allowed to live in this country? Look how thin she is." Lena was busted. Ama had discovered her ploy.

A small daycare for the children was quickly created. Among the many displaced people were those who were highly educated and some who were educators and teachers. Ama, who had developed extreme caution and a good measure of mistrust, shied away at first from other children and adults. Her friendly nature eventually prevailed, but it took time. Once she was reunited with other children her age who spoke her language and shared her interests, she relaxed and opened herself to life's experiences.

61

I do not agree with killing innocent people

The bed next to Lena's was occupied by another woman named Lizzie, who shared her cot with her daughter, Monica. The quiet young woman attracted Lena's attention. She seemed reserved and distant. At night Lena often heard her sob into her pillow.

Lena tried to engage Lizzie in conversation. "Would you like to join me on my walks? Maybe on days that Monica is playing at the preschool center? I don't go far. The fresh air and the sound of the waves calm me."

Lizzie gave Lena a long investigative stare. Not too many of the women approached her offering friendship. There was a mystery engulfing this young woman. Lena observed people give her strange looks and then engage in whispered conversations. Lena had no idea what alienated Lizzie from some of the other inhabitants.

"I was born in Frankfurt," started Lizzie as she and Lena were strolling along the pier. "Our community had 30,000 Jews. I heard that only one hundred survived.

"I was eighteen when the Nazi troops stormed into my father's shop. He was a watchmaker. I stood behind the counter. I used to help him on busy days. I did not know yet that my mother and sister had already been rounded up and taken away. I never saw them again after that cursed day. The soldiers proceeded to break the glass tops of the display cases and remove every valuable item. Two of them grabbed my father and dragged him across the floor to a truck that was parked by the shop's front door. I did not understand why they had to be so rough. He was not resisting them. I crouched down on the floor behind the counter more from shock than fear. The next thing I remember is waking up, sprawled on a dirty floor in a dark room. My head was pounding, and I felt sticky blood trickling down my face.

"I am not sure how long I lay like that in the dark, when the door to the room opened with a creak and a man dressed in the uniform of a German officer walked in. He sat down on the floor next to me and handed me a glass of water. 'You know,' he started, 'your father was shot by one of our soldiers. He did not make it into the truck. I am sorry. I don't believe in useless killing.

You are just a child, and I don't like to contemplate the future awaiting you. I am part of this army, but I do not agree with their tactics, especially the senseless killing of innocent people.' He handed me a bundle he carried and continued, 'Put this on. You will come with me. I will find a safe place for you to hide.'

"I was eighteen," continued Lizzie. "I was alone in the world and very scared. I stood up and followed him.

"Monica is his daughter. A couple of the women here are from my hometown, and they know my story. My daughter and I are viewed as contaminated. I'm viewed as a traitor and worse. They judge and loathe me. I am not excusing my actions and not apologizing for them either." She bent her head down and, with the back of her hand, wiped her tears."

Lena stopped walking, turned to the woman, and said, "A person needs to walk in the other's shoes before they choose to condemn or judge them." She grabbed Lizzie's shoulders and clung to her in a tight embrace.

62

Be a good boy and don't be afraid

Henry was a quiet, retiring boy Ama's age. He arrived alone with no family as part of a group of orphaned Jewish children. They were brought to the Marseille enclave by the Jewish social services. Ama was drawn to Henry. He seemed lonely and sad, and it touched her heart.

"How old are you?" she asked, sitting next to him on a corner bench. Henry stared down at his hands and didn't offer an answer. "Do you want me to leave you alone?" asked Ama.

"No," came a quiet reply. "I am six," Henry continued. "My birthday is in December."

"Oh," exclaimed Ama in a playful voice. "We are practically twins. Mine is in February. I am six too. Would you like to join me and my friend, Nathan, for a swim in the waterhole just outside our camp? He is a great guy. I am sure he would like you to join us."

"How do you know that he will like me?" asked Henry. His eyes revealed a story. A story of a boy forgotten, neglected, and not wanted.

"He will," assured Ama. "I promise."

Henry was from Krakow, Poland. His family went back 150 years. His father, Leib Maslowicz, worked in an iron and coal factory, providing his family with a comfortable life. Most years, Leib and his wife, Luba, enjoyed cordial relations with their Polish neighbors. They were newly married and were planning their future.

The invasion of Poland in 1939 marked the beginning of World War II. Shortly after the German invasion and occupation, the persecution of the Jews began, and Leib and Luba's lives changed forever.

A loud banging on their front door awakened them. They dressed hurriedly, listening to the loud commotion by the front door. The two couples that shared their apartment were already downstairs facing two grim-looking uniformed men. The swastikas on their arms revealed who they were.

"You are to take as few personal items as possible and gather outside by the curb," barked a heavy, red-faced officer.

"It'll be okay," Leib assured his trembling wife. "I have acquaintances in high posts, among the Germans too," he added.

"Aussteigen" (Get Out), yelled the fat officer, pushing them with the butt of his rifle.

As Luba descended from the building, forced outside her home by the officer, she noticed Hilda, her neighbor and friend. Hilda was standing with a group of neighbors. They watched in silence as their friends and neighbors were pushed and shoved into the back of a waiting truck, holding small parcels of belongings packed in a hurry. Luba looked at her friend. Hilda's eyes were cast down.

After the establishment of the Krakow Ghetto, the Jewish population was thrown out of their homes, leaving their possessions behind, and forced to live in a small, crowded section of town allocated as their new home. The ghetto was designed for exploitation, terror, and persecution. Leib and other young and able men were employed in local factories. One of these employers was Oskar Schindler, who saved the lives of 1,200 Jews by employing them in his munition factories and declaring their work essential to the war effort.

Luba and Leib shared a large room with two other couples. Eight months later, Luba gave birth to a baby boy. The cycle of life continued even in dire conditions.

Life in the Ghetto was living proof of human resilience. Synagogues were established and small classrooms where children gathered to learn the Hebrew language and the Hebrew bible. Henry loved to hear the elders pray and would not miss any occasion to join his father in his prayers.

Rumors reached them that the Nazi authorities were planning to evacuate the ghetto and transport its inhabitants to Plasfzow Concentration Camp. The function of this camp was the systematic destruction of Poland's Jewish population. Leib was aware that surviving life in the camp, especially with a young son, was not probable.

The next morning, after reaching his place of employment, Leib approached the owner of the factory. He knew the man from the time he still worked at the iron and coal factory and considered him a decent man.

Leib said to his boss, "I need you to do me a great favor. We go back a long way and we have always respected each other."

"What is it that you are asking of me?" asked his boss with some apprehension.

"My son," said Leib. "He is two years old. I need your help in saving his life. We are about to be transported to our final destination. The rumors are that it is imminent. I need to smuggle my son out of the ghetto to safety. I can pay you handsomely, and you will be doing a good deed. He is just a two-year old boy. His whole life is ahead of him." Leib's eyes were pleading. He was hoping to reach this man's sense of humanity.

Leib's boss scratched his chin and remained silent. He liked Leib and knew him as a fair, hardworking man, respected in his community. "You know what my fate will be if I am caught," he finally blurted out. Leib remained silent. Only his eyes pleaded.

Two days later Luba dressed little Henry in his warmest clothes, placed a small cloth satchel across his shoulder with some bread and cheese, and held him in a long, tight embrace. "You are my brave little boy," she said. "You are going on a trip today. *Tate (Father)* and I will join you very soon. Be a good boy and don't be afraid. I love you so much, my love." She held her tears back, handed the boy to her husband, turned around, and quickly walked away.

Leib took little Henry's small hand and walked towards the outskirts of the ghetto. He saw his boss nervously waiting at the corner of adjacent streets. A low brick wall in front obscured a motorcycle with a sidecar. Leib kissed his son on his forehead and stroked his soft brown hair.

"Look what fun you are going to have, riding in this sidecar. You climb in, and I will cover you so no one will know that you are there. It is like playing hide and seek. When Mama and I come and join you, you'll tell us all about your trip with this nice man." He instructed Henry to get into the sidecar and piled up sacks and clothes to cover the boy. He placed a small bag in his boss's hands and stepped back. The motorcycle roared and descended the road towards the gates of the ghetto. Leib's gaze followed them, tears streaming down his cheeks. "Goodbye, my sweet boy," he whispered. "Go live your life, and let it be a full and happy life. I love you."

Henry was taken to a Catholic convent. Monasteries of Nazi-occupied countries offered help in saving displaced children. One hopes that they did not lose respect for human life, and that offering refuge to Jewish children during the war was done out of compassion. There were also great concerns about the efforts of the Church to convert those children to Christianity.

After the war, Jewish organizations, looking for hidden children, did everything in their power to obtain a letter from the pope, a memorandum, asking institutions that had received Jewish children during the war years to release them into the care of the Jewish organizations that were trying to reunite them with their families. The request met with resistance from the Vatican.

Henry was taught the Catholic prayers and the sign of every pious Christian, crossing oneself. The early memories of his beginnings started to fade. They were difficult to hold on to.

One rainy morning the children were ushered to the great hall by the head nun. Henry was coming to the end of his third year in the convent. This was the only home he knew. These nuns and the other children in the orphanage were his closest thing to a family. At the age of five, the image of his parents became a distant, cloudy memory.

In the middle of the room stood a man clad in a long black coat and a black head cover. He was conversing with the head nun. "You are welcome to visit these children," said the nun. "Look at them. They are all faithful Christians. How can you tell if any of them belong to your faith?"

Rabbi Herzog smiled and stroked his long white beard. "Do not worry, dear Sister. I have my ways," he answered. He took out a white and blue fringed prayer shawl from a small cloth bag. He draped it over his shoulders, covered his eyes with his right hand, and in a strong melodious voice started to pray: "*Shema Israel, Adonai Eloheinu, Adonai Echad*" *(Hear Israel." The Lord is Our Lord. The Lord is One)*. Henry's eyes filled with tears. This was a voice from his childhood. This was a prayer he had heard twice a day recited by his father. He ran towards the rabbi and held on to his legs. More than half of the children followed.

Ama and Henry became inseparable. Lena was only too happy to have the little boy join their small family and their table for meals. Ama seemed enthralled with Henry. Her cheerful joyous mood, Lena hoped, would make her eat more.

63

We are finally going home

Palestine was an English mandate. Most surviving European Jews chose to go to Palestine, but that rout was blocked by the British who were the dominant power in that region.

They were heading towards the shores of their homeland in small, old, worn-down ships, their service retained at exuberant prices. They hoped to avoid the British authorities, who were patrolling the shores of the Mediterranean Sea. If intercepted, they were redirected to Cyprus, where another camp enclosed in barbed wire awaited their arrival.

Lena and Ama were designated to sail on a Turkish ship, engaged for the purpose of transporting displaced people to the port of Palestine, Haifa. After anxiously waiting for three months in Marseille, the anticipated day arrived.

They were about to resume their journey and embark on its last leg. Furnished with false documents, they became Mrs. Schwartz, the wife of a prominent doctor residing in Jerusalem, and their daughter, Ama. According to her documents, Lena was visiting her parents in Latvia and was trapped in Europe during the years of the war. This journey was taking her and their daughter back to their country of origin. Ama was well versed on displaying a stoic face when asked questions and avoiding giving any answers.

"We are finally going home," whispered Lena to Ama. "We'll have our own house, maybe you'll get a small dog, a girl dog, you can call her Baba. She will be all yours. No more sitting on suitcases, waiting to be told where to go next. Amichka, you were such a brave little girl through this difficult time. I am so proud of you." She squeezed her daughter's hand and wiped her own tears.

The boat was small and old. That was all the organization could afford. To Ama's delight Nathan was joining them. He got his papers too and was cleared to join them on the last leg of their trip.

The voyage was treacherous. People were holding on to the railing in fear of falling off while retching. Ama kept a close watch on her mother, watching her suffering from sea sickness with great concern. She sat next to her, holding on to her hand, as if she could bring her back to health. There was no way she would allow another person in her life to get sick, disappear or die.

On the fifth day at sea, early in the morning, Ama heard people's exclamations. The shores of Haifa were seen on the horizon. A mixture of excitement and apprehension filled everyone's hearts. Approaching their boat was an official-looking vessel. The uniformed men were signaling the boat to halt its progress.

A lengthy process of document inspection began. Lena held on to Ama's little hand and, with only her eyes, reminded her of their secret. Their paperwork, so expertly crafted by Ilka, passed the scrutiny of the investigating British officer. Lena breathed a sigh of relief. Nathan gave her a friendly wink. He passed the inspection too. They were cleared to land the next morning in Haifa, the port town.

Lena never located Nathan again after their arrival in Palestine. In such a small country, his disappearance could only have meant that his fate was the same as that of her fiancé, Ilia. She gathered that, after his arrival, he most likely joined the Jewish underground and was probably killed either by the occupying British army or by hostile forces.

64

A smell of rotting fish filled the air

Haifa is nestled between the Mediterranean Sea and majestic Mount Carmel. It is considered one of the most picturesque cities in the Middle East.

It started as a small fishing village in the third century. Along its shores, fishermen caught the murax, a sea creature whose shell, for generations, supplied a purple dye used for dying the stripes in the prayer shawls of the Jewish people.

Through the centuries, Haifa was controlled by several civilizations, including the Romans, Byzantines, Arabs, crusaders, Ottoman Turks, and the British, whose mandate was established over Palestine in 1920, after World War I.

The first and second *aliyah* (Jewish immigration) came from Eastern Europe in the early 1920s. They quickly settled into their new life and created a robust economy. By 1933, Haifa had developed into a large modern city with the most important port in the region.

Haifa was also the spiritual world center for the Bahá'i faith, a religion founded in Persia in 1840. A majestic shrine, built by the Bahá'is, graces the slopes of Mount Carmel. It is the burial site of the Báb, founder of the Bábi Faith and forerunner of Bahá'u'lláh of the Bahá'i Faith. It is considered the second holiest place on earth for Bahá'is.

The shrine was built in 1909. Its strategic placement on Mount Carmel, facing the glowing waters of the Mediterranean Sea, added to the city's majesty. It is one of the first sites a vessel approaching the shores can see. This was what Lena and Ama saw on the morning of their arrival.

"That's quite promising," thought Ama. "Maybe my vision of a majestic, sun-drenched place is coming true. Now all I hope to see is the welcoming arch."

Lena and Ama came off the boat into the welcoming arms of Lena's older brother, Eli. Ari did not come to greet his sister's arrival. He had been imprisoned by the British. He was a member of the underground resistance. They were training, preparing themselves for a troubled future. The writing was on the wall. Those arriving from a continent that had targeted and expelled them for being Jews were not welcomed. They were preparing to fight for their right to exist in their homeland.

Eli held on to Lena in a long embrace. They shed tears of joy in their reunion and sorrow for all that was lost. He bent down and looked at the little girl with the serious green eyes. "So, you are Nechama," he said in a soft voice. "I am so happy to finally meet you. I am your Uncle Eli." He kissed her lightly on her cheek and extended his hand to take hers.

Ama looked around in bewilderment. She had spent months and days creating the perfect picture in her mind of what this moment and this place would look like. It was supposed to have a tall, elaborate arch that would take her to a magical place. She would hear soft music and be surrounded by blossoming trees and singing birds. The air would smell crisp and fresh and the light engulfing her would be golden.

That was not quite the sight that welcomed her. Haifa had all the characteristics of a working port. It was June, humid and hot. The flies were buzzing around, and a smell of rotting fish filled the air. The three of them made their way, avoiding accumulated piles of discarded crates and ropes. The loud sound of two languages intermingled in the air. There were neither fragrant blossoms nor bird songs.

65

All the rooster was doing was defending his home

The word *kibbutz* in Hebrew means "*gathering.*" As a way of life, the Jewish settlers gathered and created collective communities based on agriculture. Living together and relying on each other's support ensured a safer existence.

Eli lived in such a community. Their *kibbutz* was called Kineret, named after the lake of Galilee the *kibbutz* was built next to. The lake's shape resembled a violin, *kinor* in Hebrew.

The *kibbutz* nestled in the Jordan Valley. This is where Lena and Ama landed with their worn suitcase and backpack, which were finally put aside and exchanged for a permanent, safe home.

The children in a *kibbutz* led a charmed life. Ama's love for animals and nature found this place magical. The tilled earth smelled fresh. The warm, humid air caused fragrant fruit trees and flowers to blossom furiously. She wandered across its enclosed boundaries, visiting the barns, stroking the animals. She watched in wonderment how the cows were milked and visited with Eli the large chicken coops, where he tended the flocks and invented a primitive incubator to hatch the eggs.

On one of those visits, a large, proud rooster with a blazing red comb charged at Ama and pecked her. Blood trickled down her leg. Eli aimed a swift kick at the culprit. The rooster grumbled with a loud squawk and charged again, pecking Ama in the same spot. The second kick was harder.

That evening, Eli carried home by its feet a dead rooster. Ama's love for all living creatures made her sad. All the rooster was doing, she thought, was guarding his home. He feared the stranger. For Ama, fear was a familiar sensation. She remembered times when she was ready to "peck" someone to make them stay away from her. She mourned the rooster's death.

Every day offered a new discovery. Her joyous nature and trust slowly started to return. Lena settled into a predictable life of certainty. It took a while to stop looking over her shoulder and worrying what the future held for her and Ama. She saw her daughter flourish, and that filled her with quiet joy. She was able to contribute to the joint efforts with her skills in mending and creating new clothes for the people in the community.

A large hall in the center of the *kibbutz* served as a dining hall and a gathering place for special events. People congregated there three times a day to companionably share meals and the latest news.

"How come you have this hole, right here?" Ama asked. Her Uncle Eli and she were sprawled on the soft green grass in front of the dining hall. Eli lay on his back, the sun stroking his face. Ama studied him closely. She touched the dimple in the middle of his chin.

"Oh, that," responded Eli. "Well, you see one day I was lying here on the grass after a meal, just like today. Some food crumbs left on my face attracted a large bird. It swooped down and pecked my chin. It wanted to eat the crumbs. Since then, I have had this hole." Ama stared at her uncle, considering how much of his story to believe. Eli was known for his sense of humor and aptitude for telling tall tales.

Her second uncle, Ari, lived in a nearby community, a *kibbutz* named Ein Gev. His eldest daughter, Tamar, was the girl in the photo Ama had studied when she corrected her mother about thin people being allowed to live in Palestine.

Ama was sitting on the edge of a fishpond watching her Uncle Ari, who was tending to the pools. The glistening, silvery fish were coming up to the surface to feast on the plentiful bugs and then diving back to the depths of the clear blue water. Ama was mesmerized. She longed to hold one of those hefty carps in her hands, give it a name and take it home with her as a pet.

Ari was in charge of the fishponds which the *kibbutz* had developed for its needs and for exporting fish to other areas of the country. Ama remembered Ari being absent when she and her mother had disembarked the boat upon their arrival at the port of Haifa. She remembered Eli telling Lena that their brother was in prison. "How come they put you in jail?" inquired Ama, pinning her uncle with her inquisitive eyes.

"That is an interesting story," replied Ari with a smile. "I was walking along, minding my own business," continued Ari. "I saw a rope on the ground, just lying there. Didn't seem to belong to anyone. I picked the rope up and continued walking, holding the rope in my hand. I didn't realize that there was a horse tied to the other end. I was charged with horse theft and imprisoned."

Both brothers shared a sense of humor and a talent for weaving fantasy. Ama continued to stare at her uncles with doubtful eyes.

66

In the distance the rumble of guns could be heard

The bedroom in the children's house was in complete darkness. The four children who shared the room were sprawled on their beds, asleep, tired from the day's activities. They were helping with the olive harvest, gathering the fruit into baskets. It was a tedious job, but they enjoyed the comradery and the time away from the classroom.

There was a commotion outside their building. Ama woke up first. She heard cheering and singing approaching. It slowly got closer to their building. Moments later, the door swung open. Her Uncle Eli was standing on the threshold. Lena stood beside him. Their faces were flushed with excitement and their eyes glistened with joy. They reached down and roused the children out of their sleep.

It was May 14, 1948, the day that David Ben Gurion, the head of the Jewish Agency, proclaimed the establishment of the first Jewish state in two thousand years.

Eli and three other men picked the children up and carried them on their shoulders to the loud singing of what sounded like the rest of the people of the *kibbutz*. They reached the dining hall, the gathering place for important events. On the grass in front of the building, hundreds had gathered. Some were clutching each other in a circle, dancing the *hora*, a spirited, celebratory

Israeli dance, to lively accordion music. Others were standing around the player, joining in with heartfelt singing. There were tears and laughter. People were congratulating each other. Some were on their knees, praying, expressing thanks and gratitude to a God who seemed to finally listen to his "Chosen People."

The British were withdrawing. Their mandate in the Middle East had expired. The League of Nations voted on adopting a resolution supporting the creation of an independent Jewish state.

In the distance, the rumble of guns could be heard. The fighting between Jews and Arabs broke out immediately following the British army's withdrawal earlier that day. In spite of the Arab invasion, Jews all over the world joyously celebrated the birth of their new nation. At midnight, the state of Israel officially came into being.

67

"Amichka," he whispered.
"You are so big"

The creation of a Jewish National homeland, granted by the League of Nations, was met with growing hostility by Arab nationalists who also claimed rights over the former Ottoman territories. They were attempting to prevent Jewish migration into Palestine, leading to growing Arab–Jewish tension. A full-scale war erupted on May 15, 1948, a month short of a year since Lena and Ama had disembarked from the ship in the port of Haifa. Eleven months of bliss had ended. The kibbutz came under attack. There was no time to prepare shelters for safety and protection. A ditch was dug in front of the children's home. They were instructed to run and hide in the ditch when they heard a warning siren announce an approaching air strike. The ditch was a quick attempt to ensure their safety.

Ama and her little classmates huddled in a ditch. It was close to an hour since the last sound of a siren had made them grab their small packs containing a blanket and a water bottle, as instructed, and run to lie flat in the ditch. There were sounds of explosions in the distance.

Ama, experienced with times of crisis, weighed her options. The main objective was to come out of this situation unharmed. She remembered another time she had turned to a higher power with requests for safety and promises of reciprocation. "God," whispered Ama, "you listened to me once before and helped me stay safe. I am asking you now not to let those bombs fall on my head. I will be very good and do everything my mother and my teachers ask me to do. I promise." She opened her eyes and watched the threatening planes disappearing into the horizon. "I guess there is a God," thought Ama. "And, if he is listening, I'll have to make sure to keep my promise, so I don't disappoint him."

As the attacks intensified, the children were evacuated towards the center of the country and housed in a school in Haifa. It was summer. Schools were in recess.

Ama was sitting in the makeshift dining hall with her classmates. There were only twelve of them, and they stayed close to each other among the many children brought to safety from other parts of the country. They were served their meal and she picked at her food absentmindedly. She missed her mother, who had stayed behind. She missed the cows, the chickens and the rest of the things that made her life in the *kibbutz* so special.

She heard her name and raised her gaze. Her Uncle Ilka was approaching from the doorway with spread arms and a big, joyous grin on his face. His mission in placing Jewish refugees after the war had come to an end and he had been in a great hurry to travel to Palestine and join his brothers in the fight for their homeland. His first stop coming off the boat was to see his little niece. He still had a pronounced limp as he slowly approached her table. Ama ran towards his spread arms. Ilka picked her up and held her in a long embrace. She wrapped her arms around his neck, burying her face in his shoulder, inhaling his familiar smell of tobacco and soap. Ilka was the closest thing to a father Ama had known since Michal's death when she was three.

"Amichka," he whispered. "You are so big, I can hardly hold you," he said with a wink. "I am so happy to see you," he added and planted two kisses on her cheeks.

"Are you going to stay here? With me?" she asked anxiously.

"We will all be together again very soon," he promised. "I first must go and help your uncles in the fighting." He took out a sketchbook and colored pencils from his pack and handed them to her. "You keep drawing great pictures. You can show them to me next time I see you."

Ilka didn't take much time to rest. He traveled north to join the fighting forces in Ein Gev, Ari's *kibbutz*. His skill in war tactics was invaluable, and his joining their fighting forces was greatly appreciated.

Lena worked at the *kibbutz* clothes warehouse. She enjoyed contributing her efforts to the place that had welcomed her and her daughter. The building was old, its ceiling tall, with exposed rafters. She heard a familiar sound above her and raised her eyes. A white dove was perched on a beam staring down at her, cooing softly. Through the open door she saw two official-looking men approaching the building.

"Nope," she thought to herself. "I don't think I want to meet those men, and I don't want to hear anything they have to tell me. Maybe if I just get out through the back door and walk away from here so fast they won't be able to catch up with me, maybe then, whatever they came to tell me would never have happened." Lena slipped through the back door and headed for the open fields. A dark shadow like spider webs constricted her heart. At that moment, she was willing to reconcile even with God, who had deserted her so often in the past, if only he would ensure her brothers' safety.

Ilka and Ari were guarding the perimeters of *kibbutz* Ein Gev. They were under heavy artillery attacks. The makeshift ditch, dug in haste, was their only cover. They were huddled next to each other when a hand grenade hit their ditch. Ilka was gravely injured. He died six days after arriving in the land he had helped so many people to reach. He was twenty-six.

Lena mourned her younger brother's untimely death and sank into a deep depression. "I thought they were coming to tell me that both Ari and Ilka were killed," she told Ama years later. The survival of Ari was some consolation, but not enough. She continued to mourn the loss of her baby brother, who had supported and taken care of her and Ama through the war until the time they boarded the boat that brought them to safety.

The war lasted ten months. The Jews established their right to rebuild a home for their people with hope for the cooperation of their angry neighbors. Ama and her classmates returned to their home.

68

Permanence was about to be yanked from her again

It was a crisp, sunny morning in June. Lena and Ama were taking a walk among the orange trees this region was so well known for. The air was filled with the blossoms' fragrance. Big, luscious oranges were waiting to be harvested.

Lena stroked Ama's fine hair and looked down at her daughter with apprehension. "There is something I'd like to share with you," she began. Her voice was cautious. She knew how healing this last year had been for her daughter and was hesitant about what she was about to share. "We are going to move to Haifa," she continued. "I am sure you will love your new life just as much as you love your life here. You'll meet new children and have new experiences, those of a large city."

Ama remained silent. She was not convinced of her mother's predictions about a new life. The imminent change in her future, after such a short time of settling into a trusted, safe existence, filled her with sadness. She longed for permanence, and now it was about to be yanked from underneath her again.

It was summer when they settled in their new home. School was out, and the days extended, long and boring. Ama missed her life on the *kibbutz*. She missed wandering in the fields watching the butterflies, smelling the scent of the orange trees in bloom, and visiting the cows and sheep in their barns.

Their small apartment was on the second floor, and, when she ventured into the street, all that occupied her were mounds of sand on nearby construction sites, where she built castles, dreaming she could escape her life and become a princess who lived in one of her sandcastles.

Ama learned where the trucks that drove produce from the *kibbutz* to the city were arriving. She found her way to Haifa's commercial district and stood across the street from the central office, watching the trucks from the *kibbutz* unload produce and upload supplies to be taken back.

"I wish I could hide in one of those boxes he is loading on the truck," she thought. She watched the driver disappear into the office to sign release papers. In a flash she sprinted across the busy road, climbed into the back of the truck, and pulled a heavy tarp over her head.

Her arrival at the *kibbutz* surprised her uncle and aunt. The means by which she had achieved her wish to come back were frowned upon but secretly admired. Eli hurried to call his sister to ensure her of Ama's safety.

"You can come back and visit with us as often as you'd like," said Eli. "The chickens, cows, and sheep will miss you, I'm sure," he teased her. "I'll tell you what," he added, "come with me to the chicken coop. I have a surprise for you."

69

"I hope you'll be happy here,"
said Ama to the little creature

Ama settled in the back of a bus. She was, reluctantly, heading back to Haifa after her adventurous visit. She was returning from Kineret, a place she loved and still considered her home. She chose to sit at the back of the bus, hoping that no other passenger would choose to sit next to her. The back bench was not a desirable place. That's where the bumpy road was felt the most.

She carefully opened the front of her coat and whispered, "You are safe now. I won't let anyone know that you are on the bus, but please try and keep quiet." She pushed a finger through the metal mesh of a small cage and stroked the head of a tiny yellow chick.

Her Uncle Ari, who was in charge of raising the chickens of the *kibbutz*, had sent her home with a gift, a newborn baby chick. "She misses her life with us," thought Ari. "This little chick may brighten her move to the big city."

Ama was hesitant about sharing the existence of her companion with the bus driver, not knowing if he would allow it to come along.

The new addition to the household did not fill Lena with joy. Their apartment was on the second floor, and Rosie, Ama's new pet, was assigned to the balcony, its new quarters.

"I hope you'll be happy here," said Ama to the little creature. "I will be sure to get you food, and we can visit and spend time together. I don't have friends in this place, so you'll be my friend."

Little Rosie thrived and kept Ama company; however, as weeks and months went by, it became evident that Rosie was a Ross. The young chick developed into a magnificent rooster with a proud red comb perched on its head and shiny white feathers adorning his ample body. Ama continued to share daily meaningful talks with the bird, and Ross seemed to like her. His beady eyes followed her around and he would strut towards her and hop onto her lap. The feeling of a warm small creature in her arms filled her with joy.

Ama had to climb a monumental number of steps returning home from school. Haifa is built on a mountain. Her home, nestled on a hillside, was a long climb from her school. At times, she chose the longer, more roundabout, but less strenuous route. This day she was in a hurry. A sense of doom engulfed her. She wasn't sure why. Upon entering the apartment, she threw her book bag on a chair and rushed to check on Ross. She was accustomed to hearing him crow as she approached the building but that day there were no rooster greetings in the air. Ross was not anywhere to be found. She ran outside and combed the hillside behind their building. She called his name and searched for a long time. Ama sat down on the ground and lowered her head. Ross was just a chicken, but, in Ama's short life, creating close, meaningful relationships was magical, and it didn't matter with what species or in what language

Ama returned home crying. Lena tried to comfort her daughter. "Ross was lonely, you know?" she said. "He heard the sound of chickens on the next block and chose to join them."

"How did he jump down from the second floor?" asked Ama, perplexed.

"Well, chickens have wings, you know, and they can use them when needed."

Twenty years later, when Ama was on a visit, they were sitting companionably sharing a meal in Lena's cozy kitchen. "Do you remember Ross, the rooster you raised when you were little?" asked Lena. "It was a Friday when we had Ross for our Shabbat meal," continued Lena with a mischievous glint in her eye. She believed that she was sharing a funny story with her daughter and didn't expect the reaction it brought.

"You killed my Ross?" whispered Ama. The shock in her daughter's eyes alarmed Lena. As with the story of the horses drowning in the Syr Darya River while they were crossing it and little Ama's inquiries about the horses' fate, Lena didn't share her daughter's deep concern for animals' lives. She also didn't understand the loving connection between her daughter and a chicken. She was oblivious to what that little creature had meant in the life of a lonely little girl. Ama stood up slowly and pushed her chair away from the table. She proceeded to the bathroom and promptly threw up.

70

Ama heard snickering from the back of the room

Ama walked into the classroom. It was the beginning of a school year, her first year in a new school in Haifa, where she and Lena had relocated. She was looking forward to becoming, once again, part of a group of children her age, with whom she could communicate and share her interests. The time she had spent in the kibbutz was cut short just as she started to gain confidence and trust. She yearned to be able to play and have fun just like a normal child, leaving the bad years behind, forgetting they existed. She was hoping to find a close girlfriend with whom she could giggle and share secrets.

Upon entering the room, twenty-two little faces rose and stared at her. "This is Ama," said Matilda, the teacher. "Ama comes from a faraway country. Please welcome her."

Ama heard a snickering sound from the back of the room. "She's weird," whispered a boy's voice. "Why is she dressed funny?" sounded a second voice.

This was not a good beginning. Ama, flushed and embarrassed, sat down at the desk assigned to her. She attempted to shove her large school bag into the special shelf for book bags underneath the tabletop. She heard soft chuckles across the room. Her bag was a man's large, dark-brown leather briefcase. It was difficult to fit it in the small space under the desk. Other children had small leather backpacks with straps, some in red. They were especially designed for grade-school children. Ama's book bag had been given to them by a well-wishing friend.

She was dressed in a button-down shirt with a dark cardigan over it. Her pants, sewn by Lena, had been made from the fabric of a man's grey wool dress pants. It had a herringbone weave design. Lena did her best to dress Ama in what she considered appropriate attire for her new life; however, the somber adult-looking clothes highlighted her foreignness. She was a refugee and her appearance attested to it.

School lunch break was filled with the sound of children running in groups through the yard, playing hopscotch on the pavement or sitting companionably sharing lunch. No one approached Ama. She ate her sandwich, wrapped in wax paper, sitting by herself on a small bench in a corner of the courtyard.

When the bell rang, the children rushed back into the classroom. Everyone reached for their books nestled in their book bags. Ama reached under her desk. Her book bag was gone. She looked around, puzzled and confused. She heard stifled laughter throughout the room. Her large book bag had been taken out and tossed outside into the bushes by some of her classmates.

She was taunted and called names on her walk back from school to the small apartment they shared. It was a painful time, but she prevailed.

Academic excellence was an important element in the education of Jewish children. Ama learned the language quickly. She was an eager student and soon rose to the top of her class. That gained her the teachers' respect and therefore a high social status among her peers. Within a year, she was able to pick and choose whom she trusted as friends and whom she did not.

Many years later, Zion, a boy in her class throughout grade school, shared his memories at the class fiftieth reunion. "And there was Nechama," he said. "She was the queen, and I was in love with her."

71

"They got it all wrong.
It is never good to die for anything"

Michal and Ama shared a bench in the back of the bus. They were on a trip with their class, heading north to Galilee.

Michal was a quiet sort. She was drawn to the new girl from a foreign country, fascinated by her tenacious spirit. Michal came from a strict German background, where children were not accustomed to being heard or seen. The girls took to walking home together after school. For Ama, it meant taking the longer route, but she didn't mind. Finding a friend was a gift, and she was determined to nurture it.

"So, what do you like to do when you come home from school?" inquired Ama.

"I don't know, answered Michal. "I help my mom with the housework and do my homework. How about you?"

"I have a huge book collection," answered Ama, "about a hundred books. When I finish reading them all, I just start reading them all over again. Sometimes I climb the hill behind our house and look for bugs. I love bugs. I like to watch them. Sometimes I collect a few in a jar and bring them home with me."

"Bugs?" exclaimed Michal. "My mother would never allow me to bring bugs into the house."

"I hide them," answered Ama with a smile. "Sometimes they escape, probably trying to get back to their families. I found a turtle once," she added. "My mom let me keep it. I feed him cucumber slices. He mostly sleeps behind the fridge, where it's warm, I think I'll ask my mom for a dog." Michal stared at her new friend in wonderment. A pet was not a thing she could imagine being allowed to keep.

The bus lumbered up the windy hills. It was *Yom Hazikaron*, (Memorial Day), a day dedicated to those who had lost their lives in the creation and protection of the state of Israel. They were heading to Tel Chai, the burial place of Joseph Trumpeldor, one of the early Zionist leaders who organized Jewish immigration to Palestine. He died in a fight defending his settlement. A very large statue of a lion was built on his burial site. It was a popular spot for memorial services.

Ama and her classmates gathered around the massive statue, listening to the speeches and joining in the songs. Ama's eyes landed on the prominent letters carved in the stone right under the lion's paws. It read: "*Tov Lamut Be'ad Arzeinu.*" "It is Good to Die for Our Country."

"No...no...no..." came a voice from deep inside her. "They got it all wrong. It is never good to die for anything. I know. I was close to death at times and feel very lucky that I didn't. How about writing: 'It is Good to Live for Our Country.' Yes, I would have liked that much better."

72

You didn't hear a word I said

A ma entered the small apartment they shared with Dina, a single woman who worked as a nurse at Haifa's main hospital, Rambam. Ama liked Dina, who always listened to her problems with understanding and patience. Dina knew how to embrace life despite what fate had chosen for her. She was a small woman with a severe deformity in her posture. She would give Ama used syringes to play "nurse" with her dolls. Dina was a perfect roommate for the single mother and her daughter. She was a quiet, safe presence in the apartment.

Lena sat at the kitchen table holding a cup of black tea. She drank it in the Russian fashion, sipping from a large cup, dipping a small spoon into a saucer of jam placed next to her cup. Ama, delighted to find her mother in a relaxed mood, seized the moment and sat at the table across from her. Getting Lena's attention was not an easy task. She was always preoccupied with cooking or housework.

"How was your day?" asked Ama. Lena hummed an inaudible response. "I had my essay read today in class, and Matilda, the teacher, said that it was very well written," continued Ama with the hope of engaging her mother in a conversation. Lena's beautiful blue eyes, supposedly looking at her daughter, did not see Ama. She was lost in her own world. "You didn't hear a word I said," muttered Ama with indignation.

"Yes, I did" answered Lena. "You said, 'well written.'" She could only repeat the last two words.

"You never listen to me," complained Ama, stomping out of the kitchen.

Lena, settling into a quiet predictable life, lost her youthful spirit. The fact that she survived and now lived a comfortable life only intensified her sadness and sorrow, remembering all those that didn't survive. Her thoughts and memories imprisoned her in the past, not allowing her to appreciate her life, enjoy her daughter and the fact that they were both spared. The past hovered like a dark cloud over her.

Ama's favorite time with her mother was when Lena would tell her stories about their first five years together—stories of courage and perseverance. Ama, glued to her seat, would soak up every detail, creating vivid images in her mind, partly supported by her own memories as a very young child, letting her imagination complete the rest. She adored her mother despite the lack of warmth and intimacy in their relationship, which was either cultural or a result of Lena's emotional trauma.

There was a reluctance in the Jewish tradition to praise children and demonstrate feelings of affection towards them, partly due to a superstition that your praise will attract the evil eye. Young children lacked positive feedback, which is so important for their growth and self-esteem.

Ama learned to rely on her own company. She didn't mind spending time by herself. The adventures of the heroes in the books she read were a substitute for the lack of intimate contacts in her own life. As always, she learned to adapt to what life offered her. She loved nature and spent hours observing countless small creatures and bugs that inhabited a hill next to their apartment building, losing herself in nature, blissfully alone.

On top of that hill the Bahá'i people built the most elaborate shrine adorned with a golden dome. It was the burial place of the Báb, the founder of the Bahá'i faith. Ama became a frequent visitor to the shrine. She would take off her shoes, as was the custom, leave them at the front door, and join the visiting worshipers.

73

The question came from a stranger

The way home from school was a narrow road with old apartment buildings on each side. They were built of stone from local quarries, many in the Moorish style, with colorful tiles for floors and large curved balconies.

A stone arch in front of a three-story building led to Lena and Ama's apartment. They lived on the second floor. Nadia lived on the third. Despite the one-year difference in their ages, Nadia and Ama became friends

Nadia's parents were a strange mix. Peter was a British officer, stationed in Palestine. He was a gentle, kind sort, who liked his daughter's friend and told her that their black spaniel, Blacky, to his amazement, loved Ama more than he loved his own family. That was no surprise to Ama. She was fascinated by the sweet furry creature and paid him more attention than any of his household.

Rebeca, Nadia's mother, was a Jewish woman from Hungary. Mixed marriages were frowned upon, especially if a girl married a British soldier, who was considered an enemy. Rebeca was a busybody who liked to stick her nose into everyone's business, including Lena's, which meant that the two mothers were not too fond of each other. Nevertheless, the girls bypassed their parents' differences and spent hours of play in make-believe worlds.

In a corner of their street, Abu Izchak owned a dilapidated woodshed that supplied the neighborhood with fresh fruit and vegetables as well as small odds and ends a housewife might need. His smiling face greeted the two girls approaching his stand. Ama eyed his merchandise and pointed at a pair of sunglasses, a tape measure, and a jar of facial cold cream. "I'll take these," she said to the owner with a tone of authority. "Write it in your book. My mother will pay you."

The girls proceeded up the hill behind their apartment building and settled under a tree. With the cold cream smeared on their faces and the sunglasses perched on their noses, they measured everything in sight with the newly purchased tape measure. The wrath Ama got from her mother was worth it. The make-believe world the girls created was magical.

It was only spring, but the balmy Mediterranean weather was in full form. Ama and Nadia were sitting on a low stone wall. It was too warm for any strenuous activity. Haifa is a city built on hills. Next to their building, a long stretch of stairs led to a parallel street nestled high above their street.

"Do you two lovely girls live around here?" The question came from a man dressed in a formal suit and tie. He was obviously foreign to this country. His attire and the profuse sweat stains under his armpits attested to that.

"Uh-huh," answered Ama, eying him suspiciously. She was the one short of trust.

"Great," smiled the stranger, flashing a toothy grin. "Can you come up these stairs with me and show me the street up above here?" For years to come, for the life of her, Ama couldn't understand why she went along with his request. He was an adult with a formal appearance, and it was still difficult for her to deny an adult's request.

The girls trailed behind the stranger. He continued cooing sweet words, directing them especially at Nadia, aware of Ama's cautious, suspicious nature. They stopped at a deserted building site where he motioned for Nadia to accompany him up the stairs.

This was Ama's first encounter with a sex offender. Her little friend came back downstairs pale and shaky.

"Now girls," the creep droned on. "You go back home. But walk very slowly."

Nadia started descending the stairs at a painfully slow pace. "He said we should walk slowly," she whispered to Ama.

"What did he do to you?" demanded Ama with gritted teeth.

"He touched me, down there, you know." Nadia was weeping. "Please...please don't tell my parents," she begged.

"We need to call a policeman," said Ama. "He needs to be in jail." Nadia's sobs intensified, and Ama promised to keep it as their secret forever.

74

I believe you have a guest for lunch

Lena greeted the impeccably dressed little woman, "Well, hello, Mrs. Rosenzweig," They were both standing by the front counter of their neighborhood grocery store. "I believe you have a guest for lunch today?" She added with a wink.

Mrs. Rosenzweig was the mother of Ama's new friend, Masha. Masha and Ama shared a similar childhood. They had both spent their early years in a war-torn continent. They were both refugees, survivors of the Nazi occupation, and they had escaped the grip of the Russian regime, arriving in Israel with the hope of finding a new life.

The Rosenzweig family lived in one large room divided by a wood partition, built by her father, which created a tiny kitchen. Luba, Masha's mother, cooked wonderful savory meals in their small kitchen, and Ama was a frequent addition to their table. It was not the food she craved. It was the humor and warmth that surrounded her friend's home, warmth she so lacked in her own life.

"Oh," Luba would exclaim when she heard the front door open. "Add more breadcrumbs to the ground beef," she would say with a smile. "We have a guest for lunch."

Izaak, the father, had a disfigured face. A bone disease he contracted during the war went untreated and caused the deformity. Despite his disfigurement, Izaak was blessed with a contented disposition. Appreciative of his new life, he was fiercely protective of his family and a loving father to his only child. Close, warm relationships between her girlfriends and their fathers remained forever a magical energy Ama enjoyed being close to.

In later years, the German government offered reparations to Holocaust survivors with the hope of evening the scales of history that placed them at the bottom of being considered part of humanity. "I want nothing from those whores," muttered Izaak, "but, for you," he addressed Masha, "I will fight for everything you can get from them."

Ama often escaped the sterile silence of her home, so stripped of emotions. She would run up the hill to Masha's small apartment, pretending at times, to be part of the loving family her friend was blessed with

Luba was a handsome woman with long raven hair that she wore in a bun. Her lips were always adorned with bright red lipstick, which matched her beautiful nails, always polished with bright red lacquer. She was talented in crafts and created amazing works of embroidery and knitting.

"I will make you a large, embroidered tablecloth for your wedding," she said to Ama, handing her a gift, a small, exquisite linen cloth with bright strawberries embroidered along the edges. "I feel tired these days," she added. "A small one is all I could manage."

Luba died three months later. She died of cancer, barely given enough time to enjoy a peaceful life in a new land.

75

You were a refugee, a freak

The Promised Land, the land of milk and honey, the land of eternal sunshine, a place that, for Ama, had the promise of a glorious future, proved to be different once they reached its shores.

In a place where everyone you encountered was a brother, sister, aunt, or uncle, if not by birth, then by belonging to the same tribe, Ama was faced with a startling reality. She was a refugee. She was different and therefore shunned.

Ama's cousin, Nachum, was the son of Lena's brother, Eli, who had left his home and escaped a continent about to be torn by a bloody war, while Lena, being the faithful daughter, was expected to remain behind to take care of their aging parents. Eli had four sons. Many years later, Nachum, his eldest, reminiscing with Ama about their childhood, shared with her what he believed was a funny story, "You were a refugee, a freak. I was ashamed of you and didn't want to be associated with you."

She was an old woman when she heard this from a person she had loved and trusted. The tears still came when she heard his account of their childhood. It happened so many years ago, but it still stung. It was the six-year-old Ama, still feeling the pain of rejection.

This initial experience crushed her hopes and expectations. The cruel reality of her early experience in Israel, the country of her dreams, created another scar, a second emotional scar.

Like a physical scar, which grows tough, strong tissue, so did the emotional scar. It made her strong, resilient, and determined. She vowed that she'd never let anyone diminish or dismiss her again. At the age of eight, Ama emerged from a journey through a war-torn childhood to become a warrior herself.

76

She was making sure she would not find herself alone.

It was spring of 2005. The glorious weather made nature and its creatures come alive. Lena bent over a lilac tree and smelled its fragrance. Her eyes were shut, and she was flooded with memories. The smell took her back in time. She remembered these blossoms and their insistent smell from her childhood, watching them bloom through the kitchen window of her home in Rēzekne.

"These were the trees growing around our family home," she said to Ama. "My father planted them. I love their scent."

Ama, a mother, and grandmother by now, was on a visit to her mother's home. She had arrived from a faraway country. She could visit only once a year.

They went for a stroll. They proceeded very slowly. Lena's knees had never been the same after the war and the long hours of scrubbing floors at the Russian officers' kitchen.

Lena's arm was intertwined with Ama's, more for support than friendship. She liked her daughter's visits but was always anticipating her departure and therefore not allowing herself to fully enjoy their time together.

They stopped. Lena sat heavily on a wooden bench. The rest was timely. She was getting tired.

The sun bathed them with its warm rays. Lena leaned her head on Ama's shoulder and fell asleep. Her arm stayed firmly linked in Ama's. She was holding on. She was making sure that she would not wake up and find herself alone.

Acknowledgments

I have to start by thanking my awesome family, David, for patiently listening to my rambling on with my drafts, who said that not having English as my first language makes me a better writer.

Greg for always telling me that I am a good writer and seeing tears in his eyes while reading some of the chapters in my book.

Tamar for fitting me into her unbelievably busy schedule, reading my book, marking her corrections and at the end telling me that my style of writing has merit.

Karen for asking to read my draft and telling me later how worried she was that she'd find it boring and wouldn't know how to tell me, but at the end insisting that it has to become a movie because it is so compelling

Lior, who as always, was navigating five plates in the air of her life but still finding time to listen to bits and pieces of my story as it unraveled.

Mary, my editor, who lifted my spirit with her first response to reading my book by writing me: "It's a very moving and important story."

Jan, my book designer, who with patience and guidance allowed me to express my aesthetic preferences for the visuals of my book.

Robert, who generously offered his photography expertise in manipulating the images.

Last but never the least, my sweet friend Diane who departed this world a year ago. When I shared little snippets of my life with her, she gave me a penetrating look and said "Nikki, you must write your story," and so it began. The first seed was planted.

Nikki Basch Davis

Adobe type designer Robert Slimbach has captured the beauty and balance of the original Garamond typefaces. Adobe's first historical revival, Adobe Garamond is a digital interpretation of the roman types of Claude Garamond and the italic types of Robert Granjon.